Decolonial Solidarity in Palestine-Israel

Decolonial Solidarity in Palestine-Israel

Settler Colonialism and Resistance from Within

Teodora Todorova

I.B. TAURIS
LONDON • NEW YORK • OXFORD • NEW DELHI • SYDNEY

I.B. TAURIS
Bloomsbury Publishing Plc
50 Bedford Square, London, WC1B 3DP, UK
1385 Broadway, New York, NY 10018, USA
29 Earlsfort Terrace, Dublin 2, Ireland

BLOOMSBURY, I.B. TAURIS and the I.B. Tauris logo
are trademarks of Bloomsbury Publishing Plc

First published in Great Britain 2021
This paperback edition published 2023

Copyright © Teodora Todorova, 2021

Teodora Todorova has asserted her right under the Copyright,
Designs and Patents Act, 1988, to be identified as Author of this work.

Cover image: Ramallah, West Bank. (© Dieter Telemans/Panos Pictures)

All rights reserved. No part of this publication may be reproduced or
transmitted in any form or by any means, electronic or mechanical,
including photocopying, recording, or any information storage or retrieval
system, without prior permission in writing from the publishers.

Bloomsbury Publishing Plc does not have any control over, or responsibility for,
any third-party websites referred to or in this book. All internet addresses given
in this book were correct at the time of going to press. The author and publisher
regret any inconvenience caused if addresses have changed or sites have
ceased to exist, but can accept no responsibility for any such changes.

A catalogue record for this book is available from the British Library.

A catalog record of this book is available from the Library of Congress.

ISBN: HB: 978-1-7869-9641-1
PB: 978-1-7869-9640-4
ePDF: 978-1-7869-9642-8
eBook: 978-1-7869-9643-5

Typeset by Newgen KnowledgeWorks Pvt. Ltd., Chennai, India

To find out more about our authors and books visit
www.bloomsbury.com and sign up for our newsletters.

Contents

Introduction	1
1 Theorizing the Israeli settler colony	19
2 Bearing witness to Al Nakba in a time of denial: The case of Zochrot (Remembering)	43
3 Binationalism as settler decolonization? ICAHD and the One Democratic State	65
4 Vulnerability as a politics of decolonial solidarity: The case of the Anarchists Against the Wall	85
5 The backlash to the decolonial turn: 'Delegitimizing the delegitimizers'	99
Conclusion	119
Notes	123
Bibliography	127
Index	155

Introduction

For the Palestinians the establishment of the State of Israel in 1948 and their consequent dispossession, displacement and statelessness continues to be perceived as a manifestation of ongoing European colonialism (see Bisharat 1994; Khalidi 1992, [1959] 2005; Said 1984, 1988; Shehadeh 1988; Zureik 2001) or more specifically as settler colonialism (see Sayegh [1965] 2012). Alongside existing Palestinian anti-colonial scholarship, the past decade has seen a resurgence of critical scholarship which has utilized the settler-colonial framework to describe the geopolitics of Palestine-Israel (see Bhandar and Ziadah 2016; Busbridge 2018; Salamanca et al. 2012; Svirsky 2014a, 2014b, 2017; Veracini 2010, 2013; Weizman 2017; Wolfe 2012; Shafir 2005). This scholarship has been at pains to highlight the structural nature of Israel's colonization of Palestinian land, and in turn to emphasize 'the settler' aspect as the defining mode of displacement of the indigenous Palestinian population (in particular see Veracini 2007, 2010, 2013; Wolfe 2012, 2016a, 2016b). The contemporary turn to the settler-colonial framework has allowed an emerging and growing generation of activist-scholars working on Palestine-Israel to think about decolonization as an alternative to the official conflict-management-focused peace process. This framing has allowed for the articulation of a range of rich and complex discussions concerning the making and unmaking of settler–indigenous relations in Palestine-Israel, as well as the possibility for decolonial cohabitation (for a more detailed analysis see Bisharat 2008; Busbridge 2018; Farsakh 2011).

The application of the settler-colonial label to sociopolitical relations in Palestine-Israel remains hotly contested least of all because Zionist settlement remains premised on the mythology[1] of exilic 'return' as opposed to national 'becoming' which arguably makes it distinct from other European settler-colonial projects (see Halper 2010). However, as Wolfe (2016a) argues, there is no contradiction between being a refugee or exile and being or becoming a settler colonist. Settler colonialism instead needs to be understood as 'a structure not an event' (Wolfe 2006) characterized by collective colonial accumulation (see also Bhandar 2018; Moreton-Robinson 2015). As such, what makes one a settler is not the intent to colonize but belonging to an identifiable collective which dominates and benefits from the accumulation of native land and the dispossession of the indigenous population. This collective differentiation presupposes racial thinking with race functioning as 'a classificatory concept'.

In the context of Palestine-Israel 'focusing on what race does means exploring how Zionism historically conceptualised [European] Jews as a superior race and Palestinians and Arab Jews as inferior races, leading the State of Israel to enacting racial technologies of segregation, categorization, and discrimination' (Lentin 2018: 85). Moreover, Lentin cautions against the potentially depoliticizing use of ethnicity which places emphasis on culture and language as distinguishing markers (she argues this contra Yiftachel's (2010) 'ethnocracy' thesis[2]) and insists on the centrality of race as the primary category through which to analyse Israeli settler colonialism. Race, she argues, can better help us understand the way in which intergroup diversity and settler-colonial stratification among both Israelis and Palestinians have been strategically eliminated, concealed and/or mobilized to recreate binary thinking for the benefit of the settler-colonial regime (see also Lavie [2014] 2018). She therefore reasserts the centrality of 'becoming' in the Zionist settler-colonial project. In this case 'becoming' refers to the historic and ongoing racialization process through which dominant Ashkenazi European-heritage Jews became 'white' as a consequence of their dispossession of the indigenous Palestinians and in relation to the subordinated non-white and non-European Mizrahi Jewish population (see also Allen (2012) and Stanley (2017) on the racializing process in settler-colonial pre-apartheid South Africa).

As the 'invisible' Jewish majority population, the Mizrahim have historically played a vital role in consolidating the Zionist settler-colonial project in Palestine, by replacing Palestinian indigenous labour in the immediate aftermath of the Nakba and by continuing to enact support for far right and extreme jingoistic politics in the present context. In fact, much of the contemporary ultra-religious nationalist right-wing swing in Israeli parliamentary politics can be traced to the ascendance of Mizrahi-dominated religious parties since the 1980s and more recently the ascendance of religious nationalist rhetoric within the ruling Likud Party (see Filc 2018; Grinberg 2004). Although the Mizrahi population arguably shares a common 'Arab' cultural heritage and a subordinate class position with the remnant of the Palestinian nation within Israel's borders (see Bernstein and Swirski 1982; Chetrit 2010; Lavie [2014] 2018; Massad 1996; Roby 2015; Shabi 2009; Shohat 2017), which has led some to call for class-based solidarity, the potential for solidarity between these two groups cannot be assumed. As Lana Tatour (2016b: 488–9) argues:

> Mizrahim are simultaneously both victims and perpetuators of Zionism. They are simultaneously racialised not only as inferior Arabs but also as superior Jews. The latter is no less significant than the former ... Mizrahi mobilization and activism is thus about undermining an Ashkenazi hegemony not a Zionist one. It is a struggle to expand the category of Jewish entitlement to ensure Mizrahi Jews are as privileged as Ashkenazi Jews.

The transformation of Judaism as the sin qua non of settler-citizenship (see Lavie [2014] 2018), with its explicit codification in the latest Nation State Law (see Tatour 2019), has played a key role in what Patrick Wolfe (2016a) describes as a process of 'de-racination', arguably allowing the Mizrahim to shed their 'Oriental' origins and claim supremacy by virtue of their Jewishness. However, I concur with Lentin and Lavie that the ascendance of religiosity as the binding glue of settler-colonial Jewishness does not preclude the simultaneous existence and daily reinforcement of anti-Black racism vis-à-vis the Mizrahim (see also Chetrit 2010; Roby 2015; Shohat 2017). The consequences of this racial discrimination is corporeally experienced as poverty, criminalization, labour exploitation and limited social mobility; and coupled with shouldering the burden of policing and reinforcing the violence of Israel's military occupation and the blowback from Palestinian resistance, these structural conditions block, if not eliminate, any potential for non-racialized and decolonial solidarity between the colonized and racialized settlers.

This is not, of course, the only context in which it has been noted that struggles for assimilation and civil rights by non-white and racialized migrant communities have remained within the settler-colonial logic of the elimination of indigenous sovereignty, consequently leaving the legitimacy and viability of settler-colonial structures intact and even reinforced (see Day 2015; Estes 2019; Moreton-Robinson 2015; Wolfe 2016a and 2016b). Historically, in the context of other European-dominated settler colonies such as the United States, racialized migrant populations including the enslaved and other indentured workers have embodied a very different structural position to the indigenous population. Racialized migrants are there to labour Native land for the benefit of the settler-colonial enterprise. The indigenous, on the other hand, are supposed to disappear. Therefore, when it comes to struggles for citizenship racialized migrants have tended to strive for equality with the dominant white European group, reinforcing settler-colonial possession of the land. Indigenous groups, on the other hand, have resisted formal equality precisely because it is a form of assimilation and/or elimination of Native title (see Moreton-Robinson 2015; Simpson 2017). Thus, despite the shared condition of dispossession and colonization, Wolfe (2016a, 2016b) cautions against naïve calls for solidarity which assume a natural affinity between differently racialized populations. For this very reason he insists on recuperating the discomforting binary of Native/settler as

> the existence of major differentiations within settler (and, for that matter, within Native) societies does not alter the binary nature of the Native/settler divide. The respective differentiations are of different orders. In this connection, it is important not to be misled by voluntarism. The opposition between Native and settler is a structural relationship rather than an effect of the will. The fact that enslaved people, for example, were forcibly transported against their will does not alter the structural fact that their presence, however, involuntary, was part of the process of Native dispossession. White convicts also came against their will. Does this mean that their descendants are not settlers? (Wolfe 2016b: 2)

His conclusion being a resounding no. In the context of Palestine-Israel, the involuntary arrival, in some cases, as well as a history of exploitation and racist discrimination by the European settlers, does not exclude the Mizrahim from the category of settler. Neither does this history of discrimination absolve them of complicity in the ongoing dispossession of the indigenous Palestinian population (see also Tatour 2016b). Recentring the indigenous experience in this case means paying close attention to the way in which Palestinian citizens of Israel (those who managed to remain during the Nakba) continue to be excluded from the Jewish settler-colonial order which has codified national self-determination as belonging to the settler collective (see Knesset Basic Law 2018). It also means acknowledging the continuing land appropriation and denial of basic citizenship and even human rights to the Palestinians in the Occupied West Bank (UNOCHA 2019). And this does not even begin to capture the genocidal policies in place against the Gaza Strip since 2006. The latter being the home of nearly 2 million people, with a majority under the age of 18, a place which according to the UN will become uninhabitable in 2020 (see UNCTAD 2015; United Nations: The Question of Palestine 2018). All of the above being references to the consequences of the latest legal and policy measures which come on the back of over seventy years of dispossession, ethnic cleansing and the denial of indigenous sovereignty.

In light of these injustices, the objective of this book is to contribute to the ongoing conversation about settler colonialism in Palestine-Israel and its possible decolonization by critically examining the discursive and material processes underpinning the emergence and evolution of decolonial solidarity among a section of critical Jewish-Israelis. The monograph draws on the embodied activism and reflexive thought (or the 'praxis') of three critical Israeli groups: Zochrot, Anarchists Against the Wall and the Israeli Committee Against House Demolitions (ICAHD). The concept 'critical' here refers to those individuals and organizations who acknowledge that the Jewish-Israeli side is the dominant and stronger one in the conflict, leading to a rejection of uncritical militarist and pro-state approaches and a declaration that any discussion about potential solutions to the conflict can only progress by addressing and incorporating the Palestinian narrative.

Critical Israeli groups are further differentiated from traditional Left peace groups. The latter prefer negotiation-style interfaith dialogue groups, while the former emphasize practical solidarity and co-resistance, as well as seek to articulate a radically new and different way of thinking about intercultural cohabitation in Palestine-Israel. The notion of cohabitation as 'unchosen proximity' takes into account that any joint or collaborative struggle is based on uneven power differentials. The concept of cohabitation is henceforth emphasized as the embodiment of the notion of an ethical and political commitment to plurality and equality which rejects all political projects based on national, racial or religious exclusivism (see Butler 2012). All of the activist groups examined in this book embody this ethical and political commitment to cohabitation as one of the stated goals of decolonial praxis.

Undeniably much of this joint Palestinian-Israeli critical decolonial activism is fraught with tensions and contradictions. For a start, as numerous scholars have noted (Chetrit 2010; Lavie [2014] 2018; Roby 2015; Shohat 2017), historically and in the present, critical settler activism has tended to come from the Ashkenazi middle class. On the one hand, this reinforces existing racial hierarchies within Israeli society by privileging and reinforcing the dominant role of white Israeli activism in political life. On the other hand, and quite ironically, the over-representation of a minority from within Israel's dominant European-heritage Jewish population garners accusations simultaneously of 'elitism' and 'marginality' (see Assouline 2013; Feinstein and Ben-Eliezer 2007; Kidron 2004; Shapiro 2013; Wagner 2013). I emphasize 'ironically' because there hasn't been an active Mizrahi-led anti-discrimination movement since the 1980s, and contemporary protests overwhelmingly wrap themselves in the Israeli flag, to borrow Smadar Lavie's book title to describe the tendency to demand civil rights within and in reverence to the existing dominant nationalist-Zionist settler-colonial order.

Israel's contemporary majoritarian nationalist politics are unapologetically committed to the settler-colonial project in Palestine-Israel. Within this framework, Ashkenazi-dominated critical activism can be dismissed as 'unrepresentative' and, on the extreme end, as a betrayal of working-class Jewish-Israeli interests. On the Palestinian side, joint decolonial ventures are also a minoritarian effort, with a deeply stratified colonized landscape and long-standing political divisions which have resulted in a political stalemate. Critical race-class-gender conscious analysis and a political commitment to radical and decolonial intersectional politics are necessary to at least attempt to grapple with the obstacles and opportunities for deracializing and decolonizing Palestine-Israel. Although Palestinian-Ashkenazi joint decolonial activist efforts are riven with tension and contradiction, and given their structural marginality are possibly ultimately doomed to failure, they do offer some partial answers to the question of decolonization. Studying them is therefore both relevant and necessary.

Decolonizing Palestine-Israel

In recent years, critical Israeli voices have converged with Palestinian calls for decolonization and demands for Israel to become 'a state for all its citizens'.

This has largely been in response to the failure of the official peace process, the outbreak of the second intifada and the subsequent 2005 Palestinian civil society call for Boycott, Divestment and Sanctions (BDS) against Israel until (i) the end of occupation/colonization of Arab lands, (ii) the return of the Palestinian refugees expelled in 1948 and 1967 and (iii) equal rights for Palestinian citizens in Israel.[3] This has been accompanied by a greater emphasis on, and debate over, the possibility of cohabitation in a single and/or binational state in Palestine-Israel (Abunimah 2006; Bisharat 2008; Farsakh 2011; Hilal 2007; Loewenstein and Moor 2012; Mavroudi 2010; Raz-Krakotzkin 2011; Said 2006; Tilly 2005). This in turn has placed emphasis on solidarity and 'joint-struggle' for decolonization and democratization.

Within critical Israeli settler-activist-scholarship 'decolonization' has been theorized as (i) a symbolic process of unsettling and giving up settler privilege (see Gordon 2016; Svirsky 2017; Weizman 2017) and as (ii) a material process involving the dismantling of the apparatuses of colonial occupation (Svirsky 2014a, 2014b, 2014c). Elsewhere decolonial and indigenous scholars have also theorized the task of decolonizing solidarity in settler-colonial societies as the recentring of the settler as 'a site of uncomfortable change' (see Boudreau Morris 2017, 469), and as a practice of 'a politics of accountability' (Morgensen 2014, n.p.) which acknowledges the 'beforeness' and longevity of indigenous struggle against colonization (also see Land 2015). Decolonial solidarity, therefore, needs to be understood as a process which begins with an acknowledgement of solidarity protest as located in contested indigenous sovereign space (see Land 2015) where solidarity between the settler and indigenous is premised on 'working for, towards a vision of struggle with' (Koopman 2008: 296). Decolonial solidarity requires 'a dramatic reimagining of relationships with land, people and the state' (Syed Hussan quoted in Walia, n.d., n.p.) through the bottom-up construction of 'mutual commitment and reciprocity across borders through public discourse and socio-political struggle' (Kurasawa 2004: 234). Ultimately, as indigenous scholars Tuck and Yang (2012) insist, decolonization is about the repatriation of and/or reparation for the loss of indigenous land and sovereignty. From this perspective, the role of the settler is to engage in 'decolonial solidarity' or the unmaking of settler privilege by actively participating in indigenous-led struggles against racism and colonialism and for decolonization (see Gordon 2016).

Despite the growing shift to a decolonial framing, accepting the label of 'colonizers' has been difficult for many critical Israelis. Similarly, accepting the possibility of decolonization, resulting not only in an end to Jewish privilege in Palestine-Israel, but more so the possibility of impending minoritarian status in a future Arab-Palestinian majority state, in the case of a full or partial return, is similarly experienced as problematic and undesirable. In this sense, support for a one-state solution is not a singular or unified vision. In many respects, there are as many visions as visionaries. It is for this reason, for example, that Jeff Halper (2012), ICAHD's founder, originally argued in favour of a binational state as a precondition for cohabitation, while Zochrot's earlier reflections on the Palestinian refugee return envisaged a loose federation of autonomous cultural collectivities coexisting in a future decolonized Palestine-Israel (Musih and Bronstein 2010).

This book draws on the work of Veracini (2010) to theorize Palestine-Israel as a settler-colonial relation. Veracini stresses the separate and distinct nature of settler colonialism in general, and in relation to Israel in particular which, he argues, sets it apart from both colonialism and immigration. In the case of the former, he defines colonization as a conquered polity dominated by an 'exogenous agency'; whereas migration, while sharing the aspect of displacement with settlement, is different from it in that migrants arrive and are expected to assimilate into a pre-existing and constituted political order. Settlement, on the other hand, is characterized by conquest, 'return' and an ingathering in a place in which the settler collectivity institutes a new sovereign order where they come to be in control of both the usurped/displaced indigenous population and exogenous others such as enslaved Africans in the United States or contemporary immigrants (Veracini 2010: 3–12).

Thus, while most Israelis do not see themselves as settler colonists, particularly in the case of Mizrahi migrants who arrived in the 1950s after the establishment of the state or the more recent émigrés from Eastern Europe and elsewhere, Israel as a nation-state project nonetheless bares the hallmarks of a settler-colonial enterprise. This is particularly evident in state narratives that are dominated by disavowal, one of the key characteristics of settler psychology. This includes the disavowal of any responsibility or complicity in colonialism – in Israel's case colonialism is something associated with the British Empire, not Jewish settlers; denial of any founding violence against the indigenous population,–'they just left'; and emphasis on settler innocence and suffering – 'seeking refuge from persecution' (see the various writings of Piterberg 1996, 2001, 2008, 2010).

Disavowal is further coupled with an emphasis on settler struggle, and outstanding contribution to the land, together with an appropriation of authentic indigeneity – 'return to the promised land', 'making the desert bloom' and/or 'a land without a people, for a people without a land' (see Piterberg 2001, 2008, 2010). Indeed, such narrative tropes have played a crucial role in securing Israel's settler-colonial project, from the consolidation of early Jewish settlement in Palestine and the establishment of the State of Israel (see Pappé 2006, 2011) to the present maintenance of the ongoing oppressive tripartite regime in Israel, the West Bank and the Gaza Strip (see Azoulay and Ophir 2012), as well as the denial of the Nakba[4] and the Palestinian refugees' right of return (see Pappé 2006; Peled-Elhanan 2012).[5]

Ongoing settler colonization is not only strikingly evident in the geopolitical policies and practices of the Israeli state and its bureaucracy, particularly in the West Bank, but also in Israel within its 1948 borders. An example of the latter is the official and unofficial 'Judaization' planning and resettlement policies in force in the Galilee since the 1980s, and the ongoing expulsions of the Bedouin Palestinians in the Negev/Naqab, the latter closely mirroring land expropriation in the West Bank (see Erakat 2015; Masalha 2003; Pappé 2006, 2011; Plonski 2018; Tatour 2016a). The ongoing colonization of the West Bank is particularly hard to ignore. The settlements in annexed and occupied East Jerusalem and the West Bank are illegal under International Law.[6] Judea and Samaria, as the Israeli government officially refers to the territory of the West Bank in its internal communication and military orders, are alleged 'disputed' territory, that is, the Palestinians claim it is land for their future state, but Israel also claims it as her sovereign territory.

The half a million Israeli settler colonists who reside in East Jerusalem and the West Bank are linked to Israel 'proper' through a complex and exclusive grid of roads to which Palestinians are denied access. It is possible to drive from the settler colony of Ma'ale Adumim to Tel Aviv and back without ever being given any indication that you have left Israel or entered the occupied West Bank at any point. Palestinians, on the other hand, might live in a West Bank village half of which is on the other side of the Separation Wall, where they have no legal permission to enter or visit. This obfuscated and perplexing set-up was largely made possible by the geopolitical arrangement put into place as a result of the Oslo Accords, and the emergence of Areas A, B, and C – an arrangement which absolved Israel from responsibility as an occupying power towards the Palestinian civilians under its control and gave the military-run Civil Administration unprecedented and internationally sanctioned control of most of the physical land of the West Bank (see Abu Zahra 2007; Gregory 2004; Hanafi 2009; Weizman 2007).

Alongside disavowal and geopolitical practices of displacement and resettlement, a further characteristic of settler colonialism is the elimination and/or physical or narrative replacement of the indigenous population by the settler collectivity (see Veracini 2007, 2010; Wolfe 1999, 2006). In fact, one distinguishing aspect separating pure colonialism from settler colonialism is precisely the issue of 'labour versus land'. In pure colonialism, the exogenous rulers rely on and expect servitude by indigenous labourers, often having colonized precisely for the purpose of extracting resources and labour for the benefit of the metropole and its representatives. On the other hand, while not always achievable in reality, settler colonies aspire to independence and self-sufficiency and seek to become the natives of the land.

As Shafir (2005) highlights, early Jewish settlement in Palestine was initially modelled on other colonial entities such as French Algeria. However, during the subsequent settler waves of migration a strong emphasis on self-reliance and Jewish-only labour became the dominant demand. The difficulty of maintaining a Jewish-only labour force during pre-state settlement, partly because of the small number of Jewish workers at this stage, and also due to lack of agricultural and other skills among the Yishuv population, in contrast to the plentiful and cheaper labour provided by Palestinian agricultural workers, resulted in mass discontent and union strikes by the settler population (Shafir 2005: 44–55). In the years after the state was established, and as a result of the large-scale ethnic cleansing of the indigenous Arab-Palestinian population, the above settler-only model became the dominant mode of organization, particularly in the early years of state formation. However, it was more prominently re-established in the 1990s through the policy of 'closure' vis-à-vis the Occupied Territories. Closure has only been possible with the arrival of large numbers of cheap migrant labour from Asia, Africa and Eastern Europe to replace the cheap labour previously supplied by the occupied Palestinians (Klein 2007).

The settler-colonial sovereign ability to control the population economy, composed of settler colonists, indigenous and exogenous others, has meant that the presence of exogenous others does not challenge the settler-colonial paradigm but can rather be co-opted to bolster settler supremacy in relation to the indigenous population. A similar example, though one with far worse consequences for the indigenous population, is the case of the United States where indigenous people were eliminated almost in their entirety to be replaced by claims to settler indigeneity (Smith 2012). Thus, with the elimination of most of the indigenous population of North America, the European settler colonists have been able to institute themselves as the original and authentic inhabitants and hence to maintain their right to govern in relation to later arrivals. Moreover, the virtual elimination of the indigenous population has also meant that the settler polity has had, over time, to rely on importing racialized exogenous labour in order to develop the colonial enterprise. In the pre-state period these needs were met by the labour of enslaved Africans, and indentured African-Americans, post-emancipation. Today other racialized exogenous workers such as migrant labourers from South America fulfil this role (see Smith 2012; Walia 2013).

In this respect, one of the biggest obstacles to decolonizing settler colonialism continues to be the dominance of the elimination or zero-sum paradigm,[7] in which any future remodelling of a settler-colonial society, often as a result of struggles for recognition by exogenous others, takes place within the established settler-colonial order – for example, civil rights for African Americans in the United States. Conversely, even in cases where there has not been a physical elimination of the indigenous population, decolonization has often been characterized by the flight of the European settlers, for example, in Algeria or Rhodesia/Zimbabwe (Veracini 2007). Nevertheless, there are also other less bleak examples in which settler decolonization is an ongoing process rather than a clean and brutal break with the past, such as in post-apartheid South Africa and also the often-neglected case of many South American countries where the European settler-colonial population has by and large assimilated into the indigenous population, further mixing with exogenous others, and creating a majority mestizo (mixed) population. Thus, while settler decolonization or discontinuity remains a problematic task, it is nevertheless not an impossible one.

Binationalism as a process of decolonization

Indeed, the Palestinian call for BDS against Israel is partially modelled on the South African anti-apartheid struggle, which despite its limitations continues to be one of the most successful decolonization struggles related to a settler-colonial society. Two hallmark achievements of the BDS movement have been the critical reframing of the impasse in Palestine-Israel as a civil rights struggle for freedom, justice and equality, away from the emphasis on national liberation embodied in the logic of the two-state paradigm and the rearticulation of Palestinian-Israeli civil society relations away from coexistence forums, which imply parity and symmetry between participants, to one of co-resistance against colonization and dispossession (see Svirsky 2012, 2014a). However, the demands of the BDS call have been criticized by sympathizers and opponents alike, for their lack of clarity with regard to their stated goals, which have the potential to exclude Israeli Jews (Kamel 2014), and even for a presumed underhand desire to 'delegitimise' and/or 'destroy' Israel (see Karsh 2012). The latter charge, in particular, relates to a tendency to state Israel's right to self-define as and remain an exclusive 'Jewish state', with its potential evolution into a multicultural and democratic state for all its citizens being viewed as dangerous and destructive. However, this particular perspective stems from an uncritical assumption that states have rights which supersede those of their citizens.

As Joan Cocks writes, the debate is not really about whether Israel does or does not have a right to exist but rather that 'existence rights logically do not apply to states. People can be said to have prima facie existence rights, may claim they need a state of their own to protect them. It is only once we make this conceptual distinction that we can critically assess the cogency of that claim' (2006: 25). In relation to this, this book adopts a standpoint which, in its ethico-political commitment to justice and equality, views the state as a conveyor for the actualization and security of the rights of all its citizens and residents. Hence, it is the prerogative of citizens and residents to define, in the final instance, what their state should look like. Correspondingly, a state that insists on defining its citizen body in its image and according to its political doctrine is exclusionary and undemocratic in nature and must be reframed and rearticulated as just and egalitarian.[8]

A further criticism of the implications of the BDS call for Palestine-Israel is often articulated in terms of support and commitment for the ethnocentric two-state solution as more practical and legitimate (Hermann 2005). What does the two-state solution mean in practical terms? Critics of one-state positions often dismiss these as unrealistic intellectual and/or elite visions. Yet, the parameters of the two-state solution remain disputed. The 1947 UN Partition Plan failed as a result of the 1948 War. The 1990s Oslo Accords, often seen as a historic compromise during which Israel acknowledged the Palestinians and the Palestinians reconciled themselves to Israel's presence in Palestine-Israel, never stipulated or outlined a final two-state solution (Khalidi 1997, 2006). The widely held notion that the two-state solution would be based on the 1967 occupation borders of the Gaza Strip and West Bank relies on an interpretation of UN Security Council Resolution 242 (1967), which the Oslo Accords largely ignored, relegating the issue of borders to an ever-impending final status negotiation. Moreover, although the resolution calls for Israel to withdraw from occupied lands, there is no mention of a Palestinian state, only respect for 'recognized [state] boundaries' (Article 1.ii).

The 2012 UN General Assembly vote to recognize the 1967 Occupied Territories as an independent Palestinian State was rejected by Israel and the United States and remains so at the time of writing (see AlJazeera 2012; Tharoor 2014). Coupled with continuing occupation and ongoing settler-colonial expansion in the West Bank and Gaza Strip, the widely propagated two-state solution's borders remain just as malleable as any other alternative position. Indeed, under the implied promise of the establishment of a Palestinian state, roughly coinciding with the 1967 borders, and permitting Israel to demand 'land-swaps' for its ever expanding colonial settlements, the Oslo Accords codified further annexation and the physical separation between the West Bank and Gaza Strip, and within the West Bank itself.

At the time of writing, Israel controls all of Gaza's borders (including indirectly its Rafah border crossing to Egypt), as well as its territorial waters and airspace, and is in full control of 74 per cent of land in the West Bank, leaving the Palestinian Authority, established by the Oslo Accords, in charge of the Palestinian civilian population in roughly 26 per cent of the West Bank, and in security control of a mere 3 per cent (see also Abu Zahra 2007; Ghanim 2008; Gordon 2008; Gregory 2004; Hanafi 2009; Weizman 2007, 2011). This geopolitical reality does not, of course, make the two-state solution impossible, even if for all practical purposes it appears improbable. However, given the current impasse, growing civil society considerations of one-state alternatives are not any more elitist or unrealistic than the improbable proclamations of governmental elites who espouse support for two states while ignoring the fact that at present only one side has the power to make any sort of state possible.

Therefore, a discussion of any state scenario needs to begin with an acknowledgement that the Israeli-Palestinian impasse is a struggle between two deeply unequal sides: one a settler-colonial nation state with constantly shifting yet internationally recognized sovereign and respected borders, and the other a colonized and dispossessed population dispersed across the region and elsewhere. This power disparity is perhaps most clearly articulated in the tactics of Israel and the Palestinians. Since 1948, Israel has for the most part been able to make unilateral decisions to change the geopolitical landscape of Palestine-Israel, including but not limited to population transfer, renaming and rezoning of land, military and civilian occupation and the building and expansion of internationally unrecognized settler colonies in Gaza until 2006 and presently in the West Bank (see Abu Zahra 2007; Eldar and Zertal 2007; Ghanim 2008; Gordon 2008; Gregory 2004; Hanafi 2009; Pappé 2006, 2011; Weizman 2007, 2011).

On the other hand, as a stateless people, the Palestinians have largely relied on the mercy of inter-governmental consensus, various non-violent and violent guerrilla tactics, local, national and international campaigns and, more recently, the transnational BDS campaign for civil rights in Palestine-Israel (Atran 2010; Barghouti 2011; Khalidi 1997, 2006; Qumsiyeh 2010; Said 1984, 1988, 2006). It is for this reason that examining ongoing civil society debates and visions acts as a means to give voice to the silenced Palestinian narrative and the marginalized voices of critical Israelis who reject dominant state-centric framings of Palestine-Israel. Moreover, growing one-state co-advocacy also suggests possible convergences between Palestinians and critical Israelis; or, to paraphrase Amnon Raz-Krakotzkin (2011: 21), visions of binational cohabitation point to the potential decolonization of Zionism and an alternative Jewish national existence, and de facto Jewish-Arab cohabitation, in Palestine-Israel.

The structure of the book

Chapter 1, 'Theorizing the Israeli settler colony', is contextual and conceptual in nature. It traces the problematic way in which the dominant emphasis on partition and ethnonational separation continues to shape the Israeli-Palestinian impasse and international state-sponsored commitments to the two-state solution. Utilizing a settler-colonial lens, this chapter highlights the manner in which this thinking represents tacit and overt support and commitment to Israeli settler colonialism and indigenous Palestinian dispossession, decades after colonization and racial segregation have been largely discredited as a result of successful anti-colonial struggle and decolonization in Africa and Asia, alongside the defeat of apartheid in South Africa. The chapter also examines the way contemporary Palestinian activists have drawn analogies between the South African anti-apartheid struggle in an effort to develop effective discursive and material strategies for justice in and the decolonization of Palestine-Israel. A direct consequence of this has been the emergence of the BDS movement which has inspired significant transnational support and, this book argues, is a significant catalyst for the emergence of a critical engagement with the question of decolonization among critical Israelis.

Chapters 2 to 4 should be read as documenting chronologically the emergence and evolution of a decolonial discourse among critical Israeli civil society from the period of the Second Intifada onward. Chapter 2, 'Bearing witness to Al Nakba in a time of denial', examines the centrality of Israel's 'new historians' to the validation of the suppressed narrative of the Palestinian Nakba. This chapter argues that the sociopolitical consequence of this validation has been a critical engagement with the state's settler-colonial present among some citizens. In relation to this, the chapter examines the activist practices of the Tel-Aviv based non-governmental organization (NGO) Zochrot which works to raise awareness about the Palestinian Nakba and its legacy among the Jewish-Israeli public. The chapter concludes that despite the state's resistance to civil society efforts to reconcile Jewish and Palestinian narratives of 1948, Zochrot serves as an example of critical activism which promotes the possibility for a decolonial engagement with the past and the settler-colonial present it continues to structure. This decolonial engagement has resulted in growing advocacy for decolonization and the restoration of the Palestinian right of return.

Chapter 3, 'Binationalism as settler decolonization', examines some of the ongoing critical civil society debates in relation to whether the one-state solution is the most appropriate geopolitical arrangement for decolonial justice in Palestine-Israel. The chapter examines the 2012 ICAHD's statement calling for a binational state and critically evaluates subsequent critiques of the statement by Palestinian supporters of the one-state option. Many of these debates have revolved around the extent to which Jewish-Israelis have a collective right to political self-determination in Palestine-Israel in light of the continuing denial of the Palestinian right of return and any form of Palestinian sovereignty. The chapter argues that in the eventuality of a decolonized one-state in Palestine-Israel the notion of self-determination as 'cultural rights' for the established Hebrew-speaking national community represents a more inclusive form of collective self-determination as it affirms the vital importance of Hebrew cultural and political life. Political self-determination on the other hand is an individual right that belongs to all citizens in a democratic state.

Chapter 4, 'Vulnerability as a politics of decolonial solidarity', examines the adoption of the settler-colonial framework among Jewish-Israeli and international activists who have participated in the struggle against the West Bank Separation Wall. The turn to the settler-colonial label has led to critical and radical discussions about decolonization as an alternative to the official peace process. This framing has allowed for the proliferation of debate and discussion concerned with how settler-indigenous relations in Palestine-Israel can be rearticulated and the extent to which there is any possibility for decolonial cohabitation. The chapter concludes that the widespread embrace of the settler-colonial framework has contributed to the evolution of decolonial solidarity or activists' strategic mobilization of vulnerability in opposition to settler-colonial violence.

The concluding chapter reflects on the Israeli state's increasing authoritarian resistance to critical and decolonial civil society efforts to inaugurate a more just form of cohabitation in Palestine-Israel. It concludes with a call for the need to rethink the extent to which critical local activism can reshape a violent settler-colonial state without external intervention. Moreover, in the current climate of aggressive and exclusivist geopolitics in the international arena, we are witnessing intensifying solidarity among powerful states expressed in the growing global assault on progressive civil society and transnational grassroots solidarity. Of particular relevance to this discussion being 'The Palestine Exception to Free Speech' in the United States, attempts to criminalize the boycott movement in North America and Europe, legal attempts to redefine critiques of Zionism and the State of Israel as anti-Semitism, and the use of anti-terrorism legislation in the UK to supress solidarity activism. In this instance, the key question becomes whether transnational civil society is equipped to withstand these assaults and what impact this will have on decolonial and pro-justice efforts in Palestine-Israel, and elsewhere.

1

Theorizing the Israeli settler colony

Since the inception of 'the war on terror' at the turn of the twenty-first century, the concept of 'terrorism' has become synonymous with the Palestinian struggle for decolonization. Simultaneously, state sponsored counter-terrorism strategies have come to legitimize Israel's state violence. As a consequence, popular international media representations of the Israeli-Palestinian 'conflict' often evoke images of defensive Israeli military aerial assaults in response to aggressive acts of Palestinian terrorism (see Dor 2005; Hass 2002; Philo and Berry 2004 and 2011). International media and political focus on the violent, extraordinary and spectacular nature of Palestinian political violence has resulted in a disregard for and obscures the fact that Palestinians are more likely to engage in everyday survival or popular non-violent resistance to the Occupation. The protests against the West Bank Separation Wall which are the subject of Chapter 4, alongside the emergence of the transnational movement for Boycott, Divestment and Sanctions (BDS) discussed in this chapter, are flagship examples of the long-standing history of Palestinian-led popular resistance to Occupation and colonization.

The popular erasure and disavowal of the diverse nature of Palestinian resistance to colonization and dispossession can be partly attributed to the centrality of the colonial war-making state in sociopolitical and international legal frameworks. The Westphalian framework of sovereignty dictates that all decisions pertaining to war and peace are viewed as the prerogative of the sovereign state. In this context, political violence by non-state actors or less powerful states is often designated as 'terrorism', and hence illegitimate (see Phillips 2011; Topolski 2010). Edward Said (1988) further argues that the violence carried out by non-state groups seeks to imitate state sovereignty and its claim to the legitimate use of violence/terror for political purposes. As such, organized violence, whether carried out by the state or non-state groups, tends to rely on the same statist logic of doing politics. Karatzogianni and Robinson (2010) highlight that the statist logic is further evident in the state's preference for dealing with militant organizations, whose hierarchical structures remind it of itself, rather than with more non-hierarchical and pluralistic civil society formations. This in turn traps the domain of politics in an endless cycle of violence and recrimination.

It is not inconsequential that the establishment of Europe's colonial project of domination and dispossession of non-European peoples and territory coincides with the emergence of the doctrine of Westphalian sovereignty (see Anghie 2006; Bhambra 2016; Bhandar 2018). International law has since been and continues to be an expression of the rights of colonial war-making states to settle in indigenous land and protect their territorial acquisition with the use of legitimate force. This has rendered colonized peoples' claims to self-determination and sovereignty and any indigenous resistance to colonization as 'bound by the law and yet outside its protection' (Anghie 2006: 744). International law and the state-centric decolonization projects continue to be shaped by the colonial origins of the international state system. The mandate system established by the League of Nations reinforced the notion of European colonial tutelage. The United Nations system remains embedded in this (post) colonial state-centric system of governance. The consequences for Palestine and Palestinian rights in the land has been the historic and continuing legitimation of and permissiveness towards Israel's settler-colonial project (see also Erakat 2019).

The state-centrism of the international legal and political order has meant that since 1948 Israel's state narrative has dominated understandings of the Israeli-Palestinian impasse, while the recognition of the Palestinians and their rights have been continuously reduced to a question of pending statehood. Prior to the outbreak of the First Intifada and the signing of the Oslo Accords, the dominant Zionist position on Palestine was characterized by the twin maxims of 'a land without people, for a people without a land' and Golda Meir's infamous declaration that 'there was no such thing as Palestinians' (interview in *The Washington Post* 1969). Conversely, for the Palestinians, Jewish presence in Palestine and Zionist aspirations, in particular, have been undeniable since the onset of mass Jewish immigration in the 1930s and 1940s. On the other hand, recognition of the existence of Israel has been the hardest task. The Palestinians, who had consistently rejected partition plans for Palestine from the 1930s onwards, on the basis of their majority status in Palestine,[1] found themselves dispossessed and stateless in the aftermath of the Nakba and the creation of Israel in 1948, with the overwhelming majority of Palestinians expelled outside Palestine's historic borders.

The Palestine Liberation Organization (PLO) established in 1964 by Palestinian refugees espoused 'the elimination of the Zionist entity [Israel]' and the diaspora's return to historic Palestine as its primary goal. By 1969 the PLO, reconciled with an established and settled Jewish population in Palestine-Israel, declared its objective 'the establishment of a secular-democratic state in historic Palestine' which would guarantee the rights of Muslims, Christians and Jews alike. From the 1970s onwards the PLO increasingly shifted towards a two-state paradigm, earning international recognition as 'the sole legitimate representative of the Palestinian people' in 1974 – culminating in the 1988 Declaration of Independence which accepted a two-state solution based on the June 1967 borders of Israel, the Gaza Strip and West Bank (see Khalidi 2006). The signing of the Oslo Accords signalled the first sign of Israeli recognition of the Palestinians as a nation with a claim to sovereignty. Yet, after over five decades of military occupation and illegal Jewish settlement in the West Bank and Gaza Strip the status of the Palestinians in relation to the Israeli regime remains vastly unequal.

Since the outbreak of the Second Intifada in 2000, it has been widely accepted that the Oslo Accords and US sponsored 'peace process' had come to a halt or even an end. In many respects the Oslo period leading up to the Second Intifada consolidated Israel's settler-colonial project in the Occupied Palestinian Territories (OPTs) and exasperated the oppression and exploitation of the Palestinians. From the beginning of Israel's Occupation of the Gaza Strip and West Bank in 1967 until the signing of the Oslo Accords, the Israeli economy had been heavily reliant on Palestinian labour. Hundreds of thousands of Palestinian workers from the Occupied Territories travelled every day to work in the low-waged employment sectors in Israel. The Oslo period created and consolidated Palestinian economic dependence on Israel and witnessed the beginning of the policy of 'closure': partially, then permanently, blocking Palestinian entry from the OPTs to Israel, a situation exasperated by the fragmentation of the West Bank into administrative zones

A (11 per cent), B (28 per cent) and C (61 per cent),[2] and the construction of the Separation Wall since 2002 (see Hever 2010).

> Workers couldn't work, traders couldn't sell their goods, farmers couldn't reach their fields. In 1993 per capita GNP in the occupied territories plummeted close to 30 percent; by the following year, poverty among Palestinians was up 33 percent. (Klein 2007: 433)

According to Klein (2007), the wholesale exclusion of thousands of Palestinian labourers from the Israeli economy since 1994 was possible due to two major political factors. The first factor was the unprecedented immigration of a million Jews and others from Russia and the former Soviet countries from 1993 onwards. The new arrivals were instrumental in boosting the policy of 'closure' by taking over the low-paid jobs previously done by Palestinians. Their arrival was accompanied by the migration of impressively large numbers of nuclear scientist émigrés who joined Israel's growing arms and homeland security sectors. Many of these new immigrants were relatively ignorant of the geopolitical context in which they found themselves and they subsequently made up a substantial proportion of the Jewish settler population in the West Bank because of the relatively cheap lifestyle on offer in contrast to living in Israel-proper.

The second aspect to closure, which in essence sealed the deal, for a want of a better phrase, has been the War on Terror waged by Western states post 11 September 2001. Israel's experience in fighting a long-term conflict and defusing the Second Intifada placed it in a prime position to turn its experience to profit, making it a world leader in homeland security and the fourth largest arms dealer, bigger than the UK in 2006 (see Klein 2007). Nevertheless, war profiteering, which Naomi Klein terms 'disaster capitalism', has not benefited all Israelis equally. Since 2000, the gap between the rich and poor has been steadily growing with 25 per cent of Israelis living below the poverty line and child poverty standing at 36 per cent in 2007 (Klein 2007: 436). However, this picture is complicated by the fact that Palestinian-Israelis who constitute around a quarter of Israel's citizens, despite their minority status in the polity, are disproportionately represented in the poverty statistics. By 2010 a closer examination of the above statistics shows that around half of those living in poverty in Israel were Palestinians and two-thirds of Israeli children living in poverty are Palestinian (Pappé 2011: 6).

In contrast, the Jewish settlers in the occupied West Bank and annexed East Jerusalem, whose presence in the OPTs is considered illegal under international law, enjoy a lifestyle of luxury and prosperity not just in relation to the oppressed Palestinians but also in comparison to the average Israeli who became poorer during the same period. The Israeli economist Shir Hever (2010) argues that the incentives necessary to sustain the settlements, including lucrative tax breaks, generous government subsidies and a flourishing welfare state which has been dismantled in Israel-proper, coupled with huge security and infrastructural spending, have had a heavy financial toll on the Israeli economy, the impoverishment of which is only masked by the continuous functioning of Israel's war economy (see also Hever 2019). As a consequence of these developments the ascendancy and primacy of the settlement project within Israeli politics and society has normalized the ultra-Zionist aspiration for 'Greater Israel' (territory encompassing all of historic Palestine).

Whereas occupied Palestinians were barred from entering Israel, by 2009 the number of illegal Jewish settlers in the West Bank and annexed East Jerusalem stood at over 500,000 (Central Bureau of Statistics 2009). The immediate effect of Israel's policy of closure was a sharp rise in unemployment in the West Bank, with conditions markedly worse in the blockaded Gaza Strip. In contrast, the settlements are highly subsidized by the Israeli state and can afford to pay higher wages than can be found within the rest of the West Bank and which are considerably lower than the minimum wage in Israel. By the early 2000s the more than two hundred settlements in the West Bank boasted several hundred businesses, seventeen large industrial zones and generous tax incentives, with 30,000 Palestinian workers from the Occupied Territories employed in these industrial zones.[3] Israeli labour laws which include minimum wage requirements and advanced health and safety regulations do not apply to Palestinian workers; neither does Palestinian labour law. Palestinian Trade Unions have no access to the industrial zones, and collective organization is almost impossible because the workers rely on hard to obtain security clearance permits. Furthermore, the Israeli army has been used to suppress protests over conditions. Despite the illegal and oppressive status of the settlements, and the exploitative conditions faced by Palestinian workers in the industrial zones, occupied Palestinians have almost no choice whether to work there or not (see Who Profits from the Occupation; Winstanley and Barat 2011).

Klein (2007) describes the consequences of the policy of closure as a process which rendered the Palestinians as 'surplus humanity'. Andy Clarno attributes this phenomenon to the advent of 'neoliberal apartheid' which he defines as 'a combination of extreme *inequality*, racialised *marginalization*, extensive *securitization*, and constant *crisis*' (2017: 201, original emphasis). He further warns that by making Palestinian labour redundant since the 1990s, the neoliberalization of racial capitalism has removed the few structural barriers in place against settler-colonial elimination. The rapidly deteriorating humanitarian situation in the Gaza Strip since Israel's territorial disengagement in 2005, and the departure of the Israeli settler population, is a stark manifestation of this logic (also see Puar 2017). As a consequence, in the OPTs 'there are Israeli citizens with full rights, and there are non-Israeli, non-citizens with non-rights' (Amnon Rubinstein quoted in Eldar and Zertal 2007: xx). The above combination of continuing occupation, ever-expanding Jewish settlement in the Occupied Territories, the denial of the rights of occupied Palestinians and increasing threats against Palestinian-Israelis that they will be denationalized or 'transferred' if they do not demonstrate sufficient loyalty to Israel as a 'Jewish state' (see Lentin 2018; Ravid 2010; Tatour 2019) have resulted in the charge of 'Apartheid' (see Clarno 2017; Davis [1987] 1990, 2003; Pappé 2015) and growing calls for decolonization, one expression of which is the emergence of the BDS movement in 2005.

Settler-colonial apartheid?

Mobilization around the Second Intifada brought about the unification of the struggle for equal rights of Palestinian-Israelis with that of the occupied Palestinians in the West Bank and Gaza Strip. Palestinian-Israelis in particular have been at the forefront of articulating a secular vision for a democratic decolonial state in Palestine-Israel outlined in 'The Future Vision of the Palestinian Arabs in Israel' (2006) and the 'Haifa Declaration' (2007). The authors of both documents took the unprecedented action of aligning themselves culturally and politically with Palestinians in the 1967 Occupied Territories, as well as demanding equal rights for Palestinian citizens of Israel by challenging Israel's self-definition as 'a Jewish state'.

The year 2005 also saw the launch of the transnational campaign for BDS, which gathered rapid international momentum and is presently a well-established movement with high-profile and well-publicized activities taking place across Europe and North America. A decade later the movement is facing a political backlash; a discussion of which is the subject of the book's concluding chapter. In 2008 a number of critical Israelis established BOYCOTT! (Supporting the Palestinian Call for BDS) from within. In many respects the campaign for BDS can be seen as a catalyst for the mainstreaming of the settler-colonial framework and the emergence of subsequent discourses around decolonization (see also Erakat 2015).

The BDS movement stops short of calling for a one-state solution in Palestine-Israel, however, it established and pursues three clear objectives which articulate a clear Palestinian-led conceptualization of freedom, justice and equality as (i) an end to Occupation and colonization, (ii) equal rights for the Palestinian citizens of Israel, and (iii) the implementation of the right of return of the Palestinian refugees. The campaign takes its inspiration from the successes of the anti-apartheid boycotts of South Africa as it deems that Israel is engaged in 'Apartheid practices' as defined by the 1973 International Convention on the Suppression and Punishment of the Crime of Apartheid, ratified by the United Nations General Assembly resolution 3068 (XXVIII). BDS proponents base their claim of Apartheid on Israel's discriminatory practices within the Occupied Territories, as well as empirical evidence of discrimination against Palestinians in Israel (see Abu-Saad 2019; Clarno 2017; Davis [1987] 1990, 2003; Erakat 2015; Masalha 2003; Pappé 2015). For example, they cite the fact that Israel self-defines as a Jewish state thus symbolically excluding a quarter of its citizens who are not Jewish. Moreover, 93 per cent of the land within Israel's 1948 borders is controlled by the Jewish National Fund (JNF) and the Land Authority – land which is solely reserved for Jewish-Israelis (see Pappé 2006, 2011).

Even if one excludes the disenfranchised population in the 1967 Occupied Territories from consideration, Palestinian-Israelis continue to be excluded from the dominant Jewish ethnonation. Israeli constitutional documents (see Knesset, Nationality Law 1952) make a clear distinction in relation to citizens' entitlement to rights on the basis of nationality (le'um) which is considered distinct from citizenship (ezrahut). It is for this reason, for example, that the Law of Return (1950) makes it possible for every person defined by the State of Israel as Jewish to make aliyah, literally meaning 'ascent', to Israel from anywhere in the world and be granted automatic citizenship upon arrival, while a Palestinian who left their home under conditions of war in 1948 continues to be denied the right to return.

Within the Occupied Territories, ethnonational segregation is even more glaring. From the onset of Occupation in 1967, Military Order No. 5 declared the West Bank a closed military zone resulting in a set-up whereby 'instead of internal mobility being the rule with restrictions being the exception, restrictions are the rule, and mobility – through permits – is the exception' (Abu Zahra 2007). The permit system, alongside colour-coded IDs and vehicle registration plates, hundreds of internal checkpoints and sporadic road closures restrict Palestinian movement on a daily basis. Since 2005 family unifications between Palestinians from Israel and the Occupied Territories, or the OPT and East Jerusalem have been prohibited, and reunions between residents of the Gaza Strip and the West Bank are also practically impossible.

In practice this means that a bride from Nablus cannot join her husband in Nazareth because she is not allowed into Israel, and if he moves to live with her he would lose his residency entitlements as an Israeli citizen. The situation is even more problematic for Jerusalemites who would have their blue ID revoked if they move to reside in the West Bank and would therefore be barred from re-entering Jerusalem. This policy in effect crippled the Palestinian economy and severed the geographical continuity of the Gaza Strip, West Bank and East Jerusalem and is tearing apart Palestinian families and communities. Many Palestinians faced with insurmountable violations of their right to family life and daily restrictions on their freedom of movement have chosen to leave Palestine altogether. Observers have termed the results of Israel's closure policies 'voluntary expulsion':

> Territory can be acquired by depopulating areas and using population registries, identity cards, and permit systems to zone population movement. In other words, the manipulation of forms of (non) citizenship, to displace and dispossess some people, thereby gains territory for others. (Abu-Zahra 2007: 303)

The Palestinian experience of disenfranchisement and dispossession can be contrasted with the privileged experience of Jewish settlers in the Occupied

Territories whose very presence is in direct contravention of the Fourth Geneva Convention. While Palestinians have no citizenship rights, and are subject to arbitrary and brutal military regulations, the Israeli settlers in the Occupied Territories fall under the direct jurisdiction of Israeli civilian law and receive exclusive protection by the Israeli army. The Civil Administration, the quasi-governmental body responsible for administering Palestinians in Area C, and jointly with the Palestinian Authority (PA) in Area B, grants building permits to fewer than 5 per cent of Palestinian applicants in Area C (see B'Tselem 2017; Shezaf 2020). The same institution demolishes the homes of Palestinians it has refused to grant permits to and confiscates their privately owned land for Israeli settlement expansion under the guise of military necessity (see Eldar and Zertal 2007).

> Given that Jewish colonists – but not Palestinians – in the West Bank are treated as Israelis, heavily subsidized, and given access to a complex system of colonist-only roads and land blocks, the term 'geographical separation' [used under South African apartheid] seems also rather euphemistic in this case. (Abu Zahra 2007: 314)

Taking the above into account, can there be another explanation, other than the charge of 'apartheid', for why Jewish-Israelis and Palestinians have such a markedly different experience although they reside within the same geopolitical boundaries? The dominant thesis purports that the difference lies in that the Israeli state within its internationally recognized 1948 borders is a 'democracy', while the territories occupied in 1967 continue to be governed in a 'state of exception'. The state of exception hypothesis has in particular been applied to the Gaza Strip and the West Bank since the beginning of the policy of 'closure' in the 1990s (see Gregory 2004; Zreik 2008). Proponents of Israel as a 'democracy' often contrast the experience of 'Arab-Israelis' (or Palestinians with Israeli citizenship) with occupied, non-citizen Palestinians. The former allegedly enjoy all the trappings of modern citizenship including the right to vote in and stand for elections, while the latter's citizenship rights will one day be delivered in a yet-to-be established state of Palestine somewhere in the Gaza Strip and West Bank. However, what the state of exception thesis fails to account for is why Israeli settlers in the OPT are governed by 'democratic' Israeli law while the same democratic regime is not extended to the occupied Palestinians who have lived under Israel's military rule for over fifty years. Neither does it explain why the Palestinian citizens of Israel are similarly systematically disadvantaged vis-à-vis their fellow Jewish citizens.

In many respects, the Palestinian citizens of Israel were the first Palestinians to experience Israeli military occupation. The internal military regime, which lasted until 1966, closely resembles the tactics and strategies deployed in the present day Occupied Territories: from military closure zones, arbitrary arrests, roadblocks, random ID spot-checks, curfews and house demolitions to permanent expulsions right up until 1955, this being the fate of the Palestinian Bedouin community of the Naqab/Negev in particular (see Erakat 2015; Masalha 2003; Pappé 2006, 2011; Plonski 2018; Tatour 2016a). Land confiscation and appropriation by the state authorities in the early days of the Israeli regime have also contributed to and continue to shape present day geospatial arrangements within Israel's 1948 borders. Private Palestinian land expropriated by the state was transferred to the quasi-governmental institution of the Jewish National Fund (JNF), an institution which has since 1953 acted as the legal custodian of land on behalf of the Jewish people 'for perpetuity'. An estimated 3 per cent of land in Israel serves the housing and municipal needs, such as schools and playgrounds, of Palestinians in Israel who constitute a quarter of the overall population (see Erakat 2015; Pappé 2011):

> The emerging picture is as follows: the borders of the state are almost meaningless in that being a Palestinian citizen *inside* Israel does not mean that you are part of the collective [national] project, while being a Jew living *outside* the state does not mean that you are *not* part of this project, since according to the ethos of the state (and the Law of Return), every Jew can become a citizen at any point in time. All this renders the difference between the actual and potential (Jewish) citizen marginal and blurs the concept of borders. (Zreik 2008: 140, original emphasis)

The state of exception paradigm therefore only functions if one is examining Israel's 'democracy' from the privileged perspective of Jewish citizens (see Pappé 2008b, 2011). If, on the other hand, the situation is examined in terms of Israel's relationship with its Palestinian citizens and the Palestinians in the Occupied Territories then what is revealed is 'a state of oppression' (Pappé

2008b). Within the state of oppression two parallel regimes of governance operate simultaneously: the democratic regime applied to Jewish-Israelis is characterized by the rule of law and representative parliamentary democracy; the Palestinians, on the other hand, fall under the dominion of the autocratic, unaccountable and covert operations of the secret services and military (see also Masalha 2003; Abu-Saad 2019). Pappé (2008b) further illustrates the effects of the state of oppression with the example that the majority of Jewish-Israelis are not concerned by the fact that Israel has existed in a constitutional state of emergency since its first day. This is because the state of emergency and all that it entails has never been and, they trust, will never be applied to them. The emergency only applies to the oppressed Palestinians. Drawing on Goldberg's (2002) 'racial state' and Weheliye's (2014) concept of 'racializing assemblages', Ronit Lentin (2018) has most recently theorized 'racialization' or racial stratification as central to Israel's settler-colonial order and its insistence on governing the Palestinians in a permanent state of emergency.

Moreover, as Bruyneel (2019: 454) argues utilizing the framework of apartheid has a limited utility for 'mobilizing around injustices grounded in land dispossession that are *sine qua non* of a settler colonial context'. Least of all because racial regimes of property ownership, enclosure, mass incarceration and militarism continue to be the hallmarks of other distant settler-colonial regimes such as Australia, the United States and Canada (see Allen 2018; Bhandar 2018; Dean 2019; Moreton-Robinson 2015; Tabar 2017; Tabar and Desai 2017). In response to these injustices, the mobilization of the settler-colonial framework in the struggle against Israel's colonization of Palestinian land, and in the service of the struggle for the equal rights of the Palestinian citizens of Israel, and for the implementation of the right of return of the Palestinian refugees, has contributed to the successful globalization of the Boycott, Divestment and Sanctions Movement or BDS. The next section briefly examines the role of the Israeli military, its relationship to pre-decolonial activist efforts at peace and the manner in which these efforts have contributed to the emergence of a more critical perspective among Jewish-Israeli activists who have gone on to acknowledge and accept the validity of the Palestinian perspective. This critical activism has fed into the transnational BDS movement.

Resistance from within: From militarism to refusal

The preceding discussion concerning the apartheid label highlighted the unequal rights and privileges of Israeli settlers vis-à-vis occupied Palestinians. The role of the Israeli Defence Forces (IDF), Israel's army and the institution in charge of the administration and policing of the Occupied Territories, has so far been discussed only superficially. The IDF is one of Israel's most prized institutions. The cultural and political significance and primacy of the IDF has led many commentators to remark that Israel is 'an army with a state, not a state with an army'. Military conscription is compulsory for both men and women between the ages of 18 and 21, with the historical exception of Palestinian-Israelis and sections of the ultra-Orthodox Jewish population. Following three years of conscripted service most Israelis continue to serve as IDF reservists into their early 50s. Political success in Israeli society is directly related to military prestige, with senior political roles in the civilian government being primarily occupied by former IDF Generals and other high-ranking former combatants. Moreover, with combat roles being particularly privileged, the political sphere has tended to be middle class, Ashkenazi and male dominated (see Lahav 2010; Lemish 2005; Levy et al. 2010).

As Lahav (2010) asserts the dominant institutionalized patriarchal regime in Israel is the product of the consolidation of exclusive ethnonationalism and macho-militarism. In this context, social primacy is given to 'the Jewish community', with each individual's contribution to and relationship with the community placing them in a stratified hierarchy of citizenship, which formally excludes the Palestinians in the Occupied Territories, and further excludes and marginalizes Palestinian citizens of the Israeli state. Ashkenazi soldiers have therefore traditionally been the backbone of the IDF and its elite combat units, bearing the brunt and prestige of fighting for Israel (Levy et al. 2010). However, with the growing cost of the Occupation and the many wars Israel has had to fight over the years, many young Ashkenazim have become reluctant to serve in combat roles which put their life and well-being at risk. This reluctance, coupled with growing individualization in the neoliberal era, has resulted in many young people and their families negotiating with recruiting officers for the type and nature of the work they would perform during their military service. As growing numbers of young middle-class Ashkenazim seek exemption from military service, the IDF has found itself progressively more dependent on the Mizrahim, other traditionally marginalized groups, and new migrants to maintain the Occupation.

Given that serving in combat units remains a highly privileged role within Israeli society, for many young people from minority and marginalized groups in Israel, such as the Mizrahim, Russians, the Druze and Bedouin Arabs, military service is a means to improve their life chances and gain social influence and cultural capital (see Levy et al. 2010; Mayer 2008). The emergence in 1996 and proliferation since 2016 of private pre-military academies, which are primarily national-religious but also increasingly secular and mixed in nature, has also been noted as a significant feature of contemporary Israeli militarism. The primary purpose of these academies is to support military recruitment and retention through a strict and intense educational programme which seeks to reinforce and instil a sense of national duty and an emphasis on moral conduct or 'ethical soldiering' among its students before they are about to be conscripted in the IDF (see Eastwood 2017). Some of these academies are located in West Bank settlements which underscores their tacit, if not explicit, commitment to the colonization of Palestinian land.

Despite the continuing social and political primacy of the military and combat service, it is important to note that resistance to unquestioned militarism and protracted conflict has also historically come from within the IDF ranks, and *selective refusal* has in the past been at the heart of serving and former combatants' attempts to broker peace deals prior to the contemporary decline and decimation of the mainstream Peace Now movement. Those who subscribe to selective refusal, such as the long-standing organization Yesh Gvul, emphasize the illegality and consequent social moral degeneration of Israel's Occupation of the Gaza Strip and West Bank. They subscribe to the notion that the role of a national army is primarily to defend the nation from external attack, which is the reason for the emergence of the Israeli 'refusenik' movement in 1982 following Israel's invasion of Lebanon. From this perspective Lebanon is viewed as one of the first offensive wars fought by Israel; although a clear examination of 1948 and 1967 wars places such an evaluation into question.

Peretz Kidron (2004: 55) defines 'selective refusal' as a strategy which 'places soldiers on par with the generals and politicians in judging overall policy'. In *Public War, Private Conscience*, Andrew Fiala (2010) argues for the right to refuse to be extended to professional soldiers in countries where compulsory conscription is no longer in operation. He argues that soldiers who have chosen to work in the army must not be treated as if they have surrendered their right to citizenship and, therefore, the right to object to morally objectionable policies or state actions. Both of these positions, which differ in that one refers to a professional and the other to a conscript army, share an underlying presumption that selective refusal best serves 'democratic' countries. Both allude to the role of selective refusal in bolstering and maintaining the moral and ethical character to which democracies allegedly subscribe to but on many occasions diverge from. Both of these approaches, while providing a critical and legitimate way out for non-pacifist objectors, nevertheless maintain the significance, particularly in the Israeli case, of military service and the role of the army in social and political responsibility. This is particularly evident in the following passage relating to selective refusal:

> While those [Israelis] who refuse outright to enlist leave themselves open to charges of shirking or evasion of 'national defence', the refuseniks were seasoned soldiers; in time their ranks extended to include many who had hitherto rendered distinguished service in frontline combat units. (Kidron 2004: 56–7)

As Cynthia Cockburn (2012) asserts, despite the attempt to summarize social attitudes to conscientious objection, Kidron nevertheless ends up emphasizing the cowardice, 'shirkers who are dodging their duty', of those who refuse to enlist versus the bravery and outstanding nature of soldiers, 'seasoned, distinguished fighters', who opt out of selective orders. Speck (2012) further argues that there is a problematic tendency for anti-militarist and war objectors' struggles to appropriate dominant militarist discourses of bravado and heroism. The significance and success of anti-militarist action should instead be measured not by its difficulty but by its ability to empower ordinary people by making them aware that refusal is not as difficult as it appears and can be done by anyone. In addition, Lemish (2005) makes the case that women's anti-war movements have also been traditionally marginalized and excluded from hegemonic militarized representations of conflict because they challenge the dominant social order by connecting patriarchy and political violence and, moreover, present a non-violent alternative. In this respect, Kidron's juxtapositioning of the brave soldiers who refuse selectively versus the shirkers who refuse completely is precisely an example of reappropriating militarist heroism with the consequential reaffirmation of militarist supremacy in social values. The above formulation is not unique and is in fact the rule and not the exception in terms of attitudes to refusal in Israeli society where contentious objection is seen as illegitimate and refusal is punishable by repeated imprisonment. Selective refusal, which is itself disappearing from view, as opposed to conscientious objection to war-making, continues to be one of the cornerstones of Israeli opposition to the military's role in Occupation and colonization.

Alongside the older and more established mode of selective refusal, Kidron includes a discussion of the emergence of a second generation of objectors, namely the Schminstim, or the senior high school students who signed an open declaration in 2002 that they would refuse to enlist in the 'Occupation Army'. What is striking about this generation of objectors is that they are not Kidron's seasoned fighters, on the contrary they are young people who have not yet been called up to enlist and who have and would refuse when the time comes. This generation of refusers explicitly draws analogies between 1967 and 1948 as motivating factors for their refusal and they refuse to differentiate between the two regimes of governance. As 19-year-old Alon Gurman wrote in 2012, 'My refusal to serve in the Israeli military, in addition to being a refusal to take part in Occupation and apartheid, is an act of solidarity with our Palestinian friends living under Israeli regime, and those who bravely choose to struggle against it.'[4] The Schministim draw explicit attention to the complicity of administrative and non-combatant actions within the 1948 borders of Israel in enabling the Occupation, including, but not limited to, the incarceration of Palestinian political prisoners from the Occupied Territories in Israeli prisons, as well as the development and production of weapons and military systems in Israeli academic institutions used in the Occupied Territories. Furthermore, while in the past refusal has been a primarily male issue, these young people represent a growing trend of young women refusing to enlist in the military, challenging militarist and patriarchal conceptualizations of soldiering.

In this respect the Schministim more closely resemble the position of New Profile, an anti-militarist feminist NGO which works to 'civil-ize' Israeli society, rather than the more established selective refusal movement. New Profile works towards the legitimating of conscientious objection and the establishment of a more non-violent society, highlighting the continuum between violence in the military and gendered violence in civilian society (see Cockburn 2012). They also provide support to the growing number of Israeli youth who prefer to opt out of military service on medical rather than political grounds. In this respect, contemporary trends tend to point towards the decline of refusal, particularly selective refusal, and the growing numbers of those reporting as 'unfit for service'. This has partly been attributed to young Israelis' growing unwillingness to bear the burden of serving in the army and to maintain an occupation which they do not feel has anything to do with them (see Levy et al. 2010; Mayer 2008).

The decline in the social importance of selective refusal can also be partially attributed to Nurit Peled-Elhanan's findings in *Palestine in Israeli School Books* (2012) in which she argues that the necessary education which ensures willingness to serve in the military is already well underway in school, making refusal almost unthinkable for the average 18-year-old who is conscripted shortly after high school graduation. Peled-Elhanan found that Israeli school books are characterized by a 'racist discourse' about the Palestinians which emphasizes the Jewish state and the importance of a Jewish majority. Visual or other representations of the Palestinians are almost non-existent, and when Palestinians are mentioned they are portrayed as 'primitive farmers' or 'masked terrorists'. Similarly, Palestinians are referred to as 'non-Jews' for whom there is no demographic data, or as 'foreigners'; while massacres committed by Israeli troops against Palestinians are justified and legitimated as having 'positive' outcomes for the national good. Moreover, according to Peled-Elhanan's analysis, geography books rarely show a map of Israel's real borders, referring to 'the land' rather than 'the state' of Israel, and failing to render Palestinian villages and cities within the 1948 borders, while fully depicting the Jewish settlements in the Occupied Territories. Books which do not subscribe to propagating such messages are not approved by the Ministry of Education and are either rewritten or destroyed. In essence, the education system reinforces old-standing Zionist myths about Palestine-Israel being 'a land without people for a people without land', while reducing the Palestinians to 'non-people', 'non-Jews' or 'violent and dangerous Arabs'. It is with this education and training that Israelis are conscripted into the army and sent to police and oppress the Palestinians in the Occupied Territories.

The lack of a shared narrative frame coupled with the refusal and denial of a common history continue to be two of the biggest obstacles to an ethical engagement between the Israeli colonizers and the colonized Palestinians. The next chapter examines the work undertaken by the Israeli NGO Zochrot (Remembering) which is trying to educate the Israeli public about the Palestinian Nakba in order to call for recognition, responsibility and redress for this historic and ongoing injustice. Recognition of the Nakba and the Palestinian right of return among critical and decolonial Jewish-Israeli activists has spearheaded the adoption of the settler-colonial explanatory framework and by extension the strategic importance of the transnational BDS movement for the possibility of decolonization and decolonial cohabitation in Palestine-Israel. At the core of articulating an egalitarian solution to the Palestine-Israel impasse is a commitment to the principles of justice, equality and freedom from oppression. This commitment demands mobilization across real and perceived borders of separation. The solidarity actions of Jewish-Israelis, however few in numbers they may be, serve to rupture the perceived dichotomy between Jewish-Israelis and Palestinians, signalling a breakdown of previously unquestionable pro-militarism and the unified Zionist discourse of past Israeli peace movements. The refusal to 'shoot now and cry later', something the established peace movement Peace Now was often accused of, or to separate the obvious continuities between Israeli colonialism and militarism and the Occupation ruptures the internal-Israeli consensus which is based on a logic of ethnonational unity and radical separation from the Palestinians.

Unsettling settler colonialism

Thinking about Israeli settler colonialism and the erasure of Palestinian sovereignty, as well as its necessary decolonization, also requires a critical engagement with the history and violent present of other settler-colonial contexts. Advocacy and mobilization around BDS have offered an intersectional analysis of connected struggles which inspires people to seek change and demand accountability within their local contexts, articulating the 'local' as a site of hegemonic contestation and global transformation. This has in turn contributed to the formation of cross-border solidarity between indigenous activists, racialized and colonized peoples and their decolonial and anti-racist allies from Palestine to North America and elsewhere (see Anti-Blackness Roundtable 2015; Fernandez 2017; Krebs and Olwan 2012). These transnational mobilizations for justice have given rise to demands for 'decolonial futurities' beyond settler colonialism, racial capitalism and white supremacy (see Olwan 2019; Tabar and Desai 2017), articulating the evolution of the BDS movement as a new decolonial revolutionary praxis (Roberts and Schotten 2019) or a platform for transnational solidarity politics (Dean 2019) which is rooted in locally based internationalism (Tabar 2017). BDS as a decolonial praxis is located in three key cites of practice and reflection: (i) the emergence and production of new decolonial scholarship, (ii) the emergence and rearticulation of solidarity activism as decolonial activism, and (iii) the re-emergence and rearticulation of a new transnational liberation politics.

The recent proliferation of critical settler colonial, decolonial, critical race, feminist and Marxist approaches to studying the Middle East has been central to interrogating, critiquing and articulating alternative epistemologies and methodologies for studying, analysing and envisaging alternative power relations in Palestine-Israel. This scholarship has endeavoured to displace dominant state-centric, colonial, gendered, racialized and classed discourses and to instead give voice to those who have been silenced, marginalized and excluded from self-representation and self-determination. The adoption of the settler-colonial framework within Palestine Studies (see Hawari, Plonski Weizman 2019; Salamanca et al. 2012), alongside the institutionalization of Settler Colonial Theory (SCT) and its embrace of Palestine as a pivotal case study for comparative research on historical and contemporary settler colonialism, has become widespread since the project's initiation in the early 2010s (see the various works of Wolfe and Veracini and the *Journal of Settler Colonial Studies*).

There has been some concern that the adoption of SCT, arguably in place of the anti-colonial thought that has historically characterized Palestinian liberation-focused scholarship, may result in a focus on analytical and theoretical complexity which is devoid of, or at the very least comes short of, a political commitment to decolonize. This criticism has been based on the notion that in other settler-colonial contexts, such as Australia and North America, SCT has tended to be white-dominated resulting in a body of work by settler-scholars who have been unable or unwilling to divest themselves of the internalized logics of settler colonialism. Or in other words, settler-scholars are charged with complicity in reproducing the assumption that settler-colonial dispossession is a historical event, reinforcing an acceptance of the logic of elimination which ignores indigenous resurgence and ongoing resistance to dispossession, and therefore renders settler colonialism as a triumphant (even if regrettable) project (see Macoun and Strakosch 2013).

Palestinian scholars who adopted SCT in its early stages of development have similarly been critiqued for reproducing many of the above tendencies when referring to other settler-colonial states. This has particularly been the case when Palestine is represented as an exceptional ongoing settler-colonial case engaged in a struggle for decolonization in contrast to the historical and complete nature of native dispossession in Australia and North America. This has arguably presented an obstacle for building alliances with and learning from the actual and ongoing struggles of other indigenous people. This critique has been accompanied by calls for Palestinian and decolonial scholars to align themselves with the analysis and decolonial strategies proposed by indigenous scholarship in other settler-colonial locations (Barakat 2018; Bhandar and Ziadah 2016; Salaita 2016, 2017) as a way to reaffirm the centrality of the goal of decolonization within the settler-colonial framework (see Hawari, Plonski and Weizman 2019; Macoun and Strakosch 2013; Salamanca et al. 2012; Tuck and Yang 2012).

The danger of reproducing the settler-colonial narrative of elimination by emphasizing the minoritarian status of indigenous communities in long-established settler colonies is indeed warranted. As is the criticism that it contributes to erasing ongoing indigenous activism and resistance to dispossession. Nevertheless, there are also limitations to how aspects of this critique have been framed in relation to the role of the settler-colonial framework in the study of Palestine-Israel. Firstly, without exception Palestinian, Jewish-Israeli and international decolonial scholars who have adopted the framework have done so with the vision of and commitment to liberation and decolonization, and as an initial means to destabilize the notion of Israel as a 'normal' liberal democracy. In fact, many of the aforementioned scholars are and have been active in anti-Occupation activism and the BDS movement prior to adopting the settler-colonial framework in their scholarship, having found it a far more useful analytical tool than the 'apartheid' analogy, or alternatively have joined the movement as a consequence of engaging with the framework.

Furthermore, SCT has never sought to displace or replace indigenous, anti-colonial and postcolonial theories, but on the contrary has sought to build on them and open up a space for critical and decolonial reflection on the part of settlers (see Veracini 2017). Using SCT as an analytic tool does not imply a commitment to decolonization but it does place an ethical demand to engage with the question of decolonization and its (im)possibility. This is certainly reflected in the case study chapters of this book which demonstrate that unlike in more established settler-colonial states, Jewish-Israelis, with the exception of a small critical and decolonial minority of activists and scholars, have on the whole avoided and resisted the settler-colonial label (see Halper 2010; Lentin 2018; Pappé 2008a; Sharoni et al. 2015). Resistance to the settler-colonial label is premised on its decolonial demands and its potential to serve as an advocacy and strategy tool for decolonization. Moreover, a comparative analysis of other settler-colonial states has also served to de-normalize the claims to democracy and the unquestioned legitimacy of settler sovereignty made by more established settler-colonial states. This has certainly been the case with a growing body of transnational literature linking global flows and racialized practices of incarceration, militarism, segregation and dispossession to a shared history of settler-colonial dispossession in Australia, North America and Palestine-Israel (see Al'sanah and Ziadah 2020; Collins, 2011; Tabar and Desai 2017).

The proliferation of critical scholarship which utilizes the settler-colonial framework in relation to Palestine-Israel has been intimately tied to the emergence and rearticulation of solidarity activism as a decolonial praxis. As this book outlines, this has particularly been the case for critical Jewish-Israelis. This phenomenon is examined in greater depth in relation to the Anarchists Against the Wall in Chapter 4. In the empirical context of Palestine-Israel, critical scholarship and critical activism are practically inseparable with many activists graduating to academia and many scholars having a long history of anti-Occupation activism. Scholarly-activist debates concerning settler colonialism and decolonization have also been formative and transformative for other critical NGOs such as Zochrot and ICAHD which are the subject of Chapters 2 and 3. With very rare exceptions, the so-called New Historians have been instrumental to decentring settler-colonial erasure and recentring the histories and narratives of the Palestinians. In many respects, settler-colonial theory in the context of Palestine-Israel has become a tool for decolonization by naming the problem, its structure and its possible resolution (for a more in-depth discussion of the role of decolonial pedagogy see Nakata et al. 2012).

The decolonial praxis which has emerged as a consequence of adopting and advocating for a commitment to decolonization has directly fed into and informed the re-emergence and rearticulation of a new transnational liberation politics expressed in the BDS movement. The transnational academic boycott in particular has been an expression of the radical transformation of knowledge production and intellectual pursuit as a commitment to justice and liberation (see Tabar and Desai 2017). The academic boycott has drawn into action a wide range of international academics from many disciplinary backgrounds in the humanities and social sciences including the Association for Asian American Studies, the American Studies Association and the Native American and Indigenous Studies Association in the United States.

Pegues (2016) defines these three US-based academic associations' endorsement of the boycott as an expression of solidarity which highlights international human rights violations, champions a commitment to social justice and emphasizes academic freedom as an expression of popular sovereignty and self-determination. Jakeet Singh (2019) similarly defines the academic boycott as a form of non-violent resistance, an act of individual and collective self-government and a practice of solidarity which works towards dismantling settler-colonial states. For white anti-racist allies, academic boycott initiatives have also been an opportunity for a recognition of the ways in which we are implicated in systems of oppression and domination, as well as an opportunity to build alliances across borders on the basis of accountability, mutuality and solidarity.

The proliferation of transnational boycott initiatives as well as the extent to which these initiatives have been responded to with censorship, suppression and criminalization by the Israeli state, other allied states and its right-wing civil society supporters, is a strong indication that the consensus on the legitimacy of Israel's settler colonialism is breaking down. The battle for justice in Palestine-Israel is increasingly being articulated in Gramscian terms as, on the one hand, a struggle between hegemonic acceptance of and support for settler colonialism underpinned by state-led coercion in order to maintain the increasingly fragile international consensus (also see Collins 2011). On the other hand, stands the counter-hegemonic civil society-led grassroots campaign to delegitimize and decolonize this global settler-colonial project (see also Abunimah 2014).

The movement for BDS has been an integral part of the civil society counter-hegemonic offensive. Although decolonial activism within Palestine-Israel is constituted by a minority of critical Jewish-Israelis, they have played a significant role in BDS initiatives and their contribution to the counter-hegemonic struggle is integral and indispensable to articulating a decolonial future (see also Turner 2015; Weizman 2017). The remainder of this book traces and outlines the evolution of this decolonial praxis from critical anti-Occupation activism, to a recognition of Palestinian claims for decolonization, and the emergence of a commitment to decolonization among a number of Israeli activist groups who seek to transform the current settler-colonial impasse.

Conclusion

This chapter traces the way in which Israel's Occupation of the West Bank and Gaza Strip has become entrenched in the aftermath of the failure of the Oslo Accords to deliver a two-state solution giving rise to a decolonial discourse among anti-Occupation activists. The chapter also briefly examines the history of the selective refusal movement in Israel and the limits of the success of this strategy for moving beyond the present impasse. Although the 'apartheid' analogy has been useful in highlighting the racialized and colonial nature of power relations in Palestine-Israel, the adoption of a settler colonial frame has proven far more fruitful. The ensuing transnational interconnectedness among decolonial activists has resulted in the proliferation of comparative analysis as a strategy for decolonization in Palestine-Israel. Discussions around settler colonialism have also allowed for more concrete transnational solidarity between activists in Palestine-Israel, North America, Europe and beyond.

2

Bearing witness to Al Nakba in a time of denial: The case of Zochrot (Remembering)

Since the UN decision to partition Palestine in 1947[1] and the resulting Nakba, the vast majority of Palestinians have been relegated to statelessness and exile. The Palestinians, in their millions, have for many decades spoken about the tragedy which assailed them in 1948, albeit their stories and testimonies have until recently been largely ignored within institutional discourses on the Israeli-Palestinian conflict. The dominance of Israel's state narrative has perpetuated the long-standing characterization of 1948 as a 'triumphant' war of independence during which the 'Arab' population of Palestine took 'voluntary flight' (see Peled-Elhanan 2010; Pappé 2006). The hegemonic narrative of the State of Israel has not only acted to omit Israeli perpetration of the Nakba but also has been coupled with the active denial of the very existence of the Palestinians as a national collectivity.

This political strategy dates back to early Zionist representations of pre-Jewish settlement Palestine as 'a land without people for a people without land', a claim most explicitly articulated by the Israeli Prime Minister Golda Meir, who infamously declared in a newspaper interview: 'There were no such thing as Palestinians,' proceeding to publicly deny the catastrophic events of 1947–9 by adding, 'It was not as though there was a Palestinian people in Palestine … and we came and threw them out and took their country … They didn't exist' (interview in *The Washington Post* 1969). Such acts of public denial of the existence of the Palestinians have been possible because, as Edward Said (1984: 34) writes:

> Facts do not at all speak for themselves, but require a socially acceptable narrative to absorb, sustain and circulate them. Such a narrative has to have a beginning and an end: in the Palestinian case, a homeland for the resolution

of its exile since 1948. But as Hayden White has noted in a seminal article, 'narrative in general, from the folk tale to the novel, from annals to the fully realized "history", has to do with the topics of law, legality, legitimacy, or, more generally *authority*'.

The two conflicting narratives of the events of 1948, one triumphant and one catastrophic, have been vastly unequal in terms of global public legitimacy, the former being the accepted and dominant version of 1948, while the latter has been historically absent from international debates concerning the Israeli-Palestinian conflict and the plight of the Palestinian refugees. The subject of the Nakba remains a contentious issue within international institutional discourses on the conflict because those who lay claim to having been its victims are a powerless and stateless people, while the overwhelming responsibility lies with one of the world's most influential nation states. However, since the 1980s Israel's so-called 'New Historians' have challenged linear and exclusionary historical accounts of pre-1948 Palestine as an uninhabited land, settled by the exiled Jewish people who established a state despite unrelenting opposition from its neighbours, and made the barren desert bloom.

Benny Morris's ([1987] 2004) and Ilan Pappé's (2004, 2006) works in relation to the events surrounding the state's establishment resulted in angry debates and social polarization within Jewish-Israeli society. In their differing ways, Morris and Pappé have helped to dislodge the Zionist myth[2] that Israel prior to Jewish settlement was 'a land without people for a people without land'. According to their revisionist accounts, the Palestinians did exist and lived in Palestine prior to their displacement in the war of Israel's founding and that the new Israeli state played an active role in the displacement of the indigenous inhabitants and the beginning of the Palestinian refugee problem. These new historical accounts have been part of a growing convergence between the Palestinians and a minority of critical Jewish-Israelis to rearticulate the history of the land and people of Palestine-Israel.

This chapter examines the contemporary proliferation of Israeli and Palestinian collective, individual and historical narratives concerned with the events which took place in post-Mandate Palestine and/or the newly established State of Israel between 1947 and 1949. It begins with the story of the public resurgence of the suppressed narrative of the Palestinian *Nakba* (catastrophe) after decades of silence marked by a pronounced lack of officially sanctioned narratives. The chapter continues with the story of how the Palestinians have individually and collectively held onto memories of their dispossession and how these memories have more recently been utilized politically in order to articulate the Palestinian refugees' right of return. This account is fused with a theoretical analysis of the work of the Israeli NGO Zochrot (Remembering) which seeks to reintegrate the narrative of the Nakba in the Jewish-Israeli collective consciousness by making pre-1948 Palestine and its people visible in the Israeli sociocultural and political landscape.

Zochrot's commemorative activism draws heavily on the importance of commemoration in Israeli society and a key aspect of their work involves highlighting the Nakba as Jewish-Israeli as well as Palestinian history. Their place-based practice, as will be examined towards the end of the chapter, draws heavily on Jewish commemoration of the Shoah while avoiding any direct comparisons between the two national tragedies (see Bar-On 2007; Bar-On and Sarsar 2004). Commemorating the tragedy that assailed European Jews and others during the Holocaust or Shoah has been central to the narrative of the Israeli state in terms of the importance of giving space to the voices of the victims of that historic period. For Jewish-Israelis the historic persecution of European Jews, culminating in the destruction wrought during the Holocaust, marks a distinct juncture at which the Zionist demand for a Jewish homeland in Palestine-Israel became an imperative necessity for the security and preservation of the Jewish people (see Feldman 2007). The Shoah continues to be one of the central reasons behind the state's establishment and the continuing nationalist-Zionist insistence that Israel should be and remain a Jewish nation state. The significance of the Holocaust for Jewish-Israeli communities is embodied in a range of state-sponsored commemorative practices including the establishment of Yad Vashem and the annual Yom HaShoah commemorations. As Feldman (2007) argues these commemoration practices are intimately linked to the state's commemoration of the loss of Israeli soldiers' lives and serve as a reminder of the military's importance for the safety and preservation of Jewish-Israeli communities.

The year 1948 is therefore important for both Palestinian and Jewish-Israeli narratives in two key respects. On the one hand, it marks the inauguration of the establishment of the national homeland for Jewish-Israelis. As it is argued in Chapter 3, a decolonized Palestine-Israel needs to remain a safe place for established Jewish communities in Israel and the Palestinian territories as well as those who choose to adopt Palestine-Israel as their homeland. This right should also be extended to any other migrant communities who seek to adopt the country as their home. At present, however, the Palestinians' loss of a homeland in 1948 and the continued denial of their sovereignty in the Occupied Territories and their self-determination within Palestine-Israel remain ingrained in the narratives of the Palestinians as a national catastrophe. In this respect, the 1967 Six-Day War, and the subsequent and ongoing Israeli Occupation of the Gaza Strip and West Bank, has since brought the two populations together, creating a space to potentially narrate both perspectives concerning 1948 and its legacies. Israeli organizations such as Zochrot therefore embody the importance of commemoration as a form of 'narrative reparation' (see Rosello 2010) or the importance of doing justice to another by acknowledging their sense of tragic loss.

Acknowledging and commemorating the Shoah and Nakba and their respective significance for the affected communities in Palestine-Israel should not be perceived as mutually exclusive practices and can play a key role in shifting blame away from a simple narrative of guilt/irresponsibility towards cohabitation and co-responsibility (see also Bar-On and Sarsar 2004; Boehm 2020). At present the two narratives of 1948 are perceived as competing discourses of the Jewish-Israeli and the Palestinian right to self-determination in the same territory. Yet both narratives must be acknowledged as formative of the experiences and identities of the national collectivities residing in Palestine-Israel. In addition to this, in a decolonial future there also needs to be an acknowledgement that the Shoah is a personal and integral part of the history of everyone who identifies as Jewish in Israel, in the same way as it is an important aspect of the heritage of everyone who identifies as Jewish in other countries around the world. Therefore, acknowledgement and commemoration of the victims of the Shoah and Nakba hold the key to doing justice in the present so as to work towards just decolonial cohabitation in the future. It is also important that the non-European heritage and history of the residents of Palestine-Israel is also taken into account as part of the process of decolonization (see also Shihade 2015 and 2016; Shohat 2017). Ultimately, decolonial cohabitation will require an uncomfortable and earnest reckoning with the full complexity of the histories of all constituent communities residing in Palestine-Israel.

Bearing witness in a time of denial

In *Remnants of Auschwitz*, Agamben (1999: 17) defines the *witness* as, on the one hand, a third-party observer who is called upon to testify in a court of law and, on the other, the witness (victim) 'who has experienced an event from beginning to end and can therefore bear witness to it'. In relation to the latter, Agamben argues that an ethics of witnessing is incompatible with a legal conceptualization of the witness because a separation of ethics and law becomes impossible given that, according to him, the necessary related concept of *responsibility* is already contaminated by law. Bearing witness thus becomes 'a confrontation with the infinity of responsibility' (21), thereby constituting witnessing as an impossibility. However, Catherine Mills (2003) rightly criticizes Agamben's legalistic account of witnessing for leaving out the role of the one to whom the testimony is being addressed, thereby ignoring the question of historical responsibility and its relationship to remembering and/or bearing witness (par. 21). She argues that by privileging the Latin origin of 'responsibility' in the root word 'spondeo' (to sponsor or guarantee), Agamben wilfully neglects its origin in the verb 'responso' (to reply or respond to another).

Paul Ricoeur identifies this problem as the 'duty to remember' which relates to our deep concern for the past *and* to our future orientation. The ethical responsibility 'to respond' to the testimony (account) of another is embodied in the duty to keep alive 'the memory of suffering over and against the general tendency of history to celebrate the victors' (Ricoeur 1999: 10). Here Paul Ricoeur emphasizes the role of the critical historian which is to reinforce the 'truth-claim' of memory against falsifiability *and* to revise or refute dominant history:

> In admitting what was originally excluded from the archive the historian initiates *a critique of power* [my emphasis]. He gives expression to the voices of those who have been abused, the victims of intentional exclusion. The historian opposes the manipulation of narratives by *telling the story*

differently [my emphasis] and by providing a space for the confrontation between opposing testimonies. (16)

In short, the responsibility to bear witness requires the conscious utilization of narratives which tell the dominant version of historical events 'otherwise', or in other words 'the duty to do justice, through memories, to an other than the self' (Ricoeur 2004: 89). Conversely, the alternative response to the memories of the abused and/or oppressed is *denial* or the 'need to be innocent of a troubling recognition' (Cohen 2001: 25). 'Denial is always partial; some information is always registered ... [the paradox of] knowing and not knowing' (22).

Despite the pre-existence of credible Palestinian scholarship documenting the history and geography of pre-1948 Palestine, such as the influential works of Walid Khalidi (1959 and 1992), the narrative of the Nakba began to gain widespread legitimacy within Israeli academic and political discourse only with the arrival of Israel's revisionist historians. The newly declassified IDF's archives from the 1948 war, featured in Morris's book, *The Birth of the Palestinian Refugee Problem* (1987), and the revisited edition in 2004, revealed that the over 800,000 Palestinians who 'left' Palestine during the period were in fact subjected to an organized campaign of ethnic cleansing, including forced expulsions, a number of recorded massacres and numerous cases of rape carried out by the pre-state Jewish forces against the civilian Palestinian population. Staggeringly, Morris's consecutive reflections on the very revelations he helped to bring to public knowledge have been strikingly amoral. According to Morris, his opinion reflecting the contemporary Israeli consensus, 'In certain conditions, expulsion is not a war crime. I don't think that the expulsions of 1948 were war crimes. You can't make an omelette without breaking eggs ... There are circumstances in history that justify ethnic cleansing' (interview with Shavit 2004). For Ilan Pappé, on the contrary, the dispossession of the Palestinians in 1948 by Israel represents a crime against humanity which has 'been erased almost totally from the global public memory'.

> This, the most formative event in the modern history of the land of Palestine, has since been systematically denied, and is still today not recognised as an historical fact, let alone acknowledged as a crime that needs to be confronted politically as well as morally. (Pappé 2006: xiii)

The Ethnic Cleansing of Palestine (2006) represented one of the first scholarly attempts to bear witness to the Nakba outside of the Palestinian collectivity. To bear witness is to act as a bridge between remembrance and forgetting, between memory and oblivion, between the living and those whose lives have been rendered meaningless. Bearing witness is about speaking truth to power and making an ethical and political demand for justice. Moreover, as Paul Ricoeur (2004: 500) asserts, the role of a critical historian is not only to revise and update the history of a given community, in this case the Jewish-Israeli collectivity, but to correct, criticize and even refute taken-for-granted historical narratives. As a Jewish-Israeli, Pappé's ethical stance represented an almost unprecedented and exemplary undertaking.

Pappé (2006) defined the event of 1947–9 as an organized campaign of *ethnic cleansing* by the pre-state Jewish armed forces against the indigenous civilian population of Palestine. Further, he documented the ways in which the concealment of the Nakba was achieved and continues to be maintained by the careful ideological and political efforts of the Zionist leadership and institutions of the State of Israel. Among the acts of what Pappé terms Nakba *memoricide* (2006: 225), which began in the immediacy of the ensuing state-building and power-consolidating project in the aftermath of 1948, he lists the wholesale destruction, dynamiting, bulldozing and erasing of five hundred depopulated Palestinian villages in order to prevent the return of their expelled inhabitants. Other acts of *memoricide* include the declaration of depopulated and confiscated Palestinian lands as Israeli state property, giving newly expropriated localities 'ancient' Hebrew names and handing the land over to the Israeli Land Authority for the establishment of Jewish settlements. Palestinian land was also turned over to The Jewish National Fund (JNF) for 'archaeological' and 'reforestation' programmes (Pappé 2006: 232).

> The archaeological zeal to reproduce the map of 'Ancient' Israel was in essence none other than a systematic, scholarly, political and military attempt to de-Arabise the terrain – its names and geography, but above all its history (Pappé 2006: 226) … the erasure of the history of one people in order to write the history of another people's over it. (231)

In many respects the politicization and public mobilization of the narrative of the Nakba which began in earnest during the 1990s represents a political strategy which seeks to combat Israel's concerted efforts to erase the memory of Palestinian life before 1948. In the wake of the failure of the Oslo Peace Accords, the Nakba re-emerged in the Palestinian national consciousness as a reminder of the failure of Palestinian national aspirations, resulting in a reckoning with the 'unpastness' of the past, which continues to dictate Palestinian daily existence in the form of Israel's sovereignty and Occupation versus Palestinian statelessness and absenteeism (Sa'di 2008). The ensuing proliferation of testimonies, memorial books and commemorative events in relation to the Nakba has been a collective effort to create a socially recognized narrative of the past which serves to inform the politics of the present. In many respects, the re-emergence of the narrative of the Nakba as 'a point of historical and political orientation towards the future' (Allan 2007: 253) represents an attempt to narrate the past in order to articulate the injustice, powerlessness and social exclusion experienced in the present.

Witnessing as resistance

The lack of officially sanctioned narratives and icons of commemoration due to the stateless status of the Palestinians has constituted the Nakba as a 'portable' site of memory and a temporal point of departure: 'Palestine as a birthplace, homeland, source of identity, a geographical location, a history, a place of emotional attachment and fascination, a field of imagination, and place wherein Palestinians want to end their days has dominated the lives of Palestinians on an individual and collective level' (Sa'di 2008: 387). This longing for rootedness and return is deftly narrated by Lila Abu-Lughod (2007) in her chapter in *Nakba: Palestine, 1948 and the Claims of Memory* in which she chronicles her late father's decision to return to Palestine in the wake of the Oslo Accords. She relates how from his residence in Ramallah in the Occupied West Bank he conducted regular historical 'tours' to his childhood home in Jaffa, from where his family was forced to flee in 1948.

Abu-Lughod writes that upon her father's first return visit to Jaffa, after over forty years of exile, he reported feelings of profound disorientation and unfamiliarity in the alien environment of the now Israeli suburb of Jaffa. He was nevertheless able to find his bearings and relocate himself in the city of his youth by asking local Palestinian children about the location of King Faysal Street, and to his relief they took him there immediately, even though there was no longer a sign bearing the name of that street. The children's intimate knowledge of a long expunged history and supplanted geography and Ibrahim Abu-Lughod's ability to relocate physical remnants of pre-Nakba sites, such as Hasan Bek Mosque, his now renamed and Israeli-occupied school and the now-neglected cemetery where his father's and grandfather's remains rest, testify to the living memory of the pre-Nakba years that are passed on from generation to generation through family stories.

For the Palestinian generations born after the Nakba, who derive their identities from the experience of Palestinian dispossession and statelessness, the stories and maps of the lost Palestinian villages and cities are not lived but inherited memories. These second and third generation Palestinian refugees were not born and raised in villages their parents and grandparents had to leave, nor have they had the opportunity to visit them, and even if they were permitted to return they would discover that their ancestral homes no longer exist, as they have either been reduced to ruins or are now covered by Israeli cities and settlements. Marianne Hirsch defines the above mode of formative recollection as *postmemory*

> distinguished from memory by generational distance and from history by deep personal connection ... Postmemory characterises the experiences of those who grew up dominated by narratives that precede their birth, whose own belated stories are evacuated by the stories of the previous generation shaped by traumatic events ... Postmemory – often obsessive and relentless – need not be absent or evacuated: it is as full and as empty, certainly as constructed, as memory itself. (1997: 22)

Mapping the erased and suppressed geography of former Palestinian inhabited localities is an integral part of the Palestinian endeavour to retrieve and retain the material significance of their loss: their homes, mosques, villages and lands. Rochelle Davies's (2007) account of the memorial books compiled by Palestinian refugees in the camps of Lebanon, Syria, the West Bank and Gaza Strip illustrates precisely the integral role played by the refugees' preoccupation with preserving the memories of the physical localities from which these communities were expelled or forced to flee in 1948 and have since been prevented from returning to. The compulsion and intricate detail with which these maps are drawn and communally preserved, detailing not only significant landmarks and geological habitat but also the ownership of homes and lands, is intimately tied to the Palestinian longing for and desire to return to the familiarity and ownership of their former homes.

The village, with its connotation of intimate connection to the land, remains a key site of identification and a source of belonging for the refugees who continue to organize camp life and dwelling on the basis of their localities of origin in pre-1948 Palestine. Nevertheless, the Nakba is not simply an act of recall, the experience of being uprooted from one's habitat is a tragic reality even for the subsequent generations of those Palestinians who remained within the 1948 borders of the State of Israel and for whom dispossession continues in the present. These Palestinians who are Israel's 'Arab minority', who managed to remain and received Israeli citizenship in the aftermath of 1948, although they are no longer subject to the military rule imposed on them until 1966, continue to reside in a legal and existential limbo. They are citizens of a country which treats them as 'present absentees'[3]: second-class citizens whose lands continue to be confiscated by the state, and who are denied the right of return to their former homes and localities which, unlike the refugees beyond Israel's 1948 borders, they can visit, touch and smell, but they cannot reclaim (see Abu-Lughod and Sa'di 2007; Pappé 2006).

Yet, like the children who took Ibrahim Abu-Lughod to King Faysal Street, despite nearly fifty years of absence from Jaffa's landscape, these Palestinians keep the memory of pre-Nakba Palestine alive. Palestinian Israelis organize annual processions to the localities of former Palestinian villages to commemorate the Nakba; these Marches of Return often coincide with Israel's Independence Day[4] celebrations and constitute an act of resistance in the face of denial and attempts at outright legalized repression. The 'Nakba Law' passed in 2011 makes it illegal for institutions which 'undermine the foundations of the state and contradict its values' to receive any public funding (Khoury and Lis 2011). Peled-Elhanan (2010) illustrates the anti-Nakba law in action. She writes in relation to the Israeli government's reaction to a school textbook by Domka et al. which was recalled immediately after publication because it rendered the Palestinian version regarding the ethnic cleaning in 1948 alongside the Israeli one, as a 'version' and not 'propaganda', using both Israeli and Palestinian sources (such as Walid Khalidi's books). The change requested by the ministry of education was first of all to remove the Palestinian sources from the Palestinian version and to substitute it with Palestinian texts that are 'more faithful to reality' or with Israeli sources ... In order to have the book republished, the publishers replaced the Palestinian sources with Israeli ones in the part called The Palestinian Version and gave it a lesser weight, without changing the structure. (Peled-Elhanan 2010: 398)

Despite the fierce attempts by the right-wing Israeli establishment to silence the voices of the Palestinians, the unrelenting force of the narrative of the Nakba is increasingly penetrating the consciousness of growing numbers of progressive Jewish-Israelis who are confronting the Zionist myths of their upbringing. This confrontation began with the work of Israel's New Historians and continues to articulate itself in the work of the Israeli NGO Zochrot (Remembering) whose activists work to raise awareness about the Nakba within Israeli society. In light of the historic and ongoing exclusion of Palestinian narratives from the Israeli education system, alongside the surveillance, suppression and persecution of Palestinian educators and students (see Abu-Saad 2019), the teaching of Palestinian narratives by critical and decolonial Jewish-Israeli scholars, teachers and activists serves as a decolonial praxis which unsettles the narratives of Israeli settler colonialism through critique and advocacy.

Decolonizing settler memory

Since 2002 *Zochrot* has worked to educate the Israeli public about the history and legacy of the Nakba in Hebrew. The activities of the Tel Aviv-based NGO Zochrot include public commemorative tours to the locations of the Palestinian villages destroyed during 1947–9. These tours are accompanied by the publication of booklets dedicated to these erased localities. The booklets contain history about and maps of the village, as well as testimonies from the village's refugees, and on occasion include written reflections by the Jewish-Israelis who live or have lived in the towns and settlements erected on the lands of the former Palestinian villages. Zochrot's commemorative activities echo the village memorial books compiled by Palestinian refugees in the camps as the organization routinely engages in the remapping of Palestine onto the amnesiac Israeli landscape. The NGO's tours often culminate with the erection of street signs bearing the pre-1948 names of the destroyed Palestinian villages in Arabic and Hebrew. These commemorative and educational activities exemplify what Karen E. Till (2008) theorizes as a socially engaged and ethically responsible 'place-based practice', a mode of operation based on the conceptualization of social memory as embodied experience, 'places are embodied contexts of experience, but also porous and mobile, connected to other places, times and peoples' (2008: 109).

The organization also engages in advocacy activities which seek to democratize the public landscape of Israel. These activities include actively opposing building plans which will erase the remains, without marking the existence, of depopulated Palestinian villages, such as Zochrot's successful 2006 Supreme Court lawsuit against the JNF which calls for the erection of public signs identifying the Palestinian villages on which JNF sites are now located (see Zochrot 2006a and 2006b). At the time of the original request, Zochrot's demand was widely publicized in the liberal media with numerous articles appearing in the Israeli daily *Ha'aretz*. Attempts to preserve the physical traces of the former Palestinian presence are often met with evasion and vandalism, a case in point being JNF's refusal and delay in repairing and replacing the damaged signs in Canada Park which testify to the destroyed Palestinian villages (see Zochrot 2009). Nevertheless, the battle for and against Nakba remembrance continues to be waged publicly, legally and politically, making it increasingly more difficult for the opponents of the narrative to refute its potency and moral entitlement.

Commemorative practices such as the public display of signs bearing witness to the former presence and current absence of the Palestinians, two unspeakable facts, are deeply unsettling to the Jewish-Israeli collectivity which refuses to acknowledge the past so as to avoid confronting responsibility in the present. Such commemorative acts are deeply disturbing because they 'prompt us to think about forms of descendancy, genealogies of proprietorship and histories of citizenship, and remind us that we need to reconceptualise received ideas of identity, belonging and the civic' (Jonker in Till 2008: 109). Thus, in spite of the hostile and unreceptive environment and the concerted efforts to silence the remembrance, and even utterance, of the Nakba, Zochrot's work is opening up a valuable space for Jewish-Israelis to be able to begin to confront the founding myths of Zionism, such as the notion that there was no such thing as Palestinians or Palestine, and perhaps be able to begin, at a later stage, to take ethical responsibility in order to pave the way for cohabitation.

Nakba remembrance carves out a space which enables the painful past of Palestine-Israel to be confronted with a view to acknowledge and assimilate the Nakba as a shared historical experience, an act which has the potential to enable the possibility of the two collectivities to begin to envisage a future based on decolonial cohabitation. The public commemorative events in which Zochrot engages act as a bridge between the two conflicting narratives and are opportunities for decolonial dialogue between Jewish-Israelis and Palestinians. These acts serve to democratize and reconstitute social memory not only through education and commemoration but also by posing important and challenging political questions in the form of Zochrot's 2008 public conference on the Israeli recognition of the Palestinian refugees' right of return. The conference was held at the Zionists of America House in Tel Aviv, and the location of this historically unprecedented event can be read as a sign of the Nakba narrative's power of subversion and disruption of the Zionist account and simultaneously as a testament to the flexibility and strength of the Zionist hegemony.

Such inherent contradictions in the geopolitical space within which Zochrot functions serve to illustrate the validity of some of the criticisms levelled at the organization by Lentin, who argues that much of Zochrot's work remains at the level of the symbolic, and further, activities such as mapping the land as it existed before 1948 epitomize a recolonization of Palestine (2008: 217). For Lentin this constitutes an appropriation of Palestinian memory which perpetuates Palestinian victimhood and Israeli authority. While there is validity in her criticisms, Lentin leaves little room for self-reflexivity among Zochrot activists. One of the challenges represented by her is the need for Jewish-Israelis to develop political strategies for advocating the Palestinian return – a question which was first put at the organization's aforementioned conference in 2008 and which forms part of a larger ongoing project on the practicalities of return in conjunction with the Palestinian NGO BADIL.[5]

Co-authored projects, such as the exhibition 'Towards a Common Archive' (2012) which deals with the Palestinian refugees' return, are a prime example of a critical strategy to bridge the convergent narratives of 1948 and to work towards redressing the survivors of the Nakba.

The second challenge posed by Lentin, which she admits is much more difficult, is to document the testimonies of Jewish-Israelis involved in the Nakba. Given the current climate of denial, this task is much more problematic and any progress is likely to be painstakingly slow. Nevertheless, since 2010 there has been a growing number of testimonies on Zochrot's website from former Jewish-Israeli combatants who fought in 1948 who have reluctantly come forward to speak about carrying out and/or witnessing expulsions of the Palestinians (see also Lia Tarachansky's *Seven Deadly Myths*, 2011). When I first began studying Zochrot's work in the summer of 2009, the only testimonies from 1948 available on their website were two short documentary films by the Palestinian-Israeli activist Raneen Jeries. One of the films features the testimonies of five Palestinian women who lived through and survived the Nakba. The second features two internally displaced Palestinian-Israeli survivors of the 1947 ethnic cleansing of Manshiyyah.

While Lentin (2008) criticizes Zochrot's possession of these testimonies as a form of recolonization of Palestinian memory, Zochrot activists saw their work differently. Similarly to Peled-Elhanan (2012), they stress that for an Israeli organization aimed at the Jewish public in Israel, to archive the stories of Palestinian survivors is also vitally important in order to counteract the silencing and absence of the Palestinian narrative from the Israeli curriculum, an absence which serves to continually justify hatred and violence against the Palestinian people, whether under Occupation or elsewhere. The recording of Israeli former combatant testimonies relating to 1948 begun around 2010. However, the process of recording these testimonies was rather slow in gathering momentum as most Jewish-Israelis who fought in 1948 were reluctant to come forward and speak about what they saw or did. The testimonies of former Jewish combatants who took part in the expulsions of Palestinians in 1948, collected as part of the 2012 'Common Archive' exhibition, are characterized by evasion and partial recollection. For example, sometimes it is not clear whether the former fighters are recollecting atrocities they witnessed or perpetrated (see Zochrot website for examples); similarly, there is little indication of remorse or regret for their actions, and even less desire to redress the Palestinian refugees' demand for return. In fact, many of the testimonies are reminiscent of Benny Morris's infamous remark, 'You can't make an omelette without breaking eggs.'

Nevertheless, the collection of former combatant testimonies from 1948 is absolutely vital in order to combat the officially sanctioned amnesia and denial in relation to the Nakba which characterizes Israeli society at present. Moreover, in the absence of Palestinian narratives about 1948 from the Israeli curriculum, Zochrot's website can serve as an alternative online archive which challenges the state narrative of 1948 in a manner that represents all involved constituents similarly to the achievements of the Northern Irish peace process. Simultaneously, the corroboration of Palestinian survivor testimonies through the juxtapositioning of testimonies by Jewish-Israelis who were involved in the events serves to reinforce the present necessity to recognize, take responsibility for and redress the rights of the Palestinian survivors and descendants of the Nakba. In light of the ongoing settler-colonial regime of violence and dispossession characterizing Palestine-Israel, acknowledgement in the form of recognizing the truth claims of the Palestinian narrative of the Nakba does not in itself represent an adequate response to the Palestinian call for justice. What is at stake in relation to having information about formative past events is not so much the accumulation and possession of knowledge but rather what to do with the knowing:

> The mutually performative effects that narratives and subjects have in the presence of each other sometimes produce effects that resemble what we used to call authorial intention. In this context, the interest of assuming the performativity of narrative as subject-forming moments or places and also as effects of the subject's attempt to give an account of themselves is to reframe the debate about the use, abuse or abusive (re)construction of national pasts. (Rosello 2010: 25)

In other words, the task at hand is not a question of acknowledgement but rather it is about the responsibility entailed by the recognition of the Palestinians' right to redress. The responsibility entailed calls forth not only a reframing and/or a retelling of an expunged history as a shared history, but also a reframing of the subject positions of the settled and long-standing communities in Palestine-Israel. Responsibility calls for a reframing of victims and perpetrators, or the colonized and colonizer, in a manner that honours the role of the past in the present relation of dispossession, misrecognition and violent irresponsibility. In essence, the task at hand is to articulate a future-oriented vision of cohabitation and co-responsibility between Jewish-Israelis and Palestinians living in Palestine-Israel, as well as of those who wish to return and remain. The 'Common Archive' project is therefore an example of a future-oriented project that not only serves as a testament and acknowledgement in the present moment of what was done in 1948 but can also act as a catalyst to a truth and reconciliation process in the future.

Indeed, much of Zochrot's work since around 2012 has been inspired by the work of the Truth and Reconciliation Commission (TRC) in South Africa. A joint study visit by BADIL and Zochrot activists in 2012 led to the publication of the 'The Cape Town Document' which lays out a joint vision for the Palestinian refugees' return and was presented and discussed at the second Right of Return Conference, held at Boston University, the United States in April 2013. Bearing in mind critiques of the TRC process, Zochrot and BADIL have focused their efforts on redress rather than truth. One of the biggest criticisms levelled at the TRC has been its individuation of the crimes committed during the Apartheid regime which allegedly detracted from the need for collective reparation (Mamdani 2002). The misplaced focus on truth for amnesty at the expense of atonement and the redress of the collective experience of injustice has in turn been criticized for leaving the socio-economic framework of apartheid in place in post-apartheid South Africa, with continuing white minority control of land and resources and the growing deprivation and dispossession of the black majority (Clarno 2017; Valji 2003).

It is for this reason that the Cape Town return 'vision document' focuses not only on Israeli acknowledgement and corroboration of the Nakba, but more significantly on the recognition of the right of return, taking responsibility for its implementation or lack thereof and consequently the question of redress. Significantly, the authors of the vision paper assume a post-Zionist future in which the return will take place. However, there is no indication or discussion of how this post-Zionist future is to be arrived at, or what the role of the activists might be in bringing about this post-Zionist moment. Although the paper is unique and unprecedented in scope and nature as it is the first time Jewish-Israelis and Palestinians have got together to actively think and plan the Palestinian refugee return, the document nevertheless remains contradictory in many places. For example, the authors admit that there are major unresolved disagreements over a two- or one-state solution, an issue which is likely to have a major impact on the return and its nature and scope. Similarly, there is great disagreement over the question of property restitution and rights. For example, are the current Jewish-Israeli occupiers of properties that belonged to Palestinians who were expelled or left in 1948 to be evicted from these properties, or are the original Palestinian owners to be compensated instead? In either case, do the Jewish residents have any rights to property and/or compensation if they had purchased in good faith and/or lived there for a prolonged period of time? This has to be taken into consideration given the time which has lapsed since 1948.

The document also provides numerous 'track' options for individual and collective return and attempts to resolve some underlying inequalities in Palestinian society. For example, it argues that financial and practical provisions for return should also be made for those refugees and their descendants who left behind land and property as well as for those who did not have land and/or property but are nevertheless entitled to compensation and financial redress. These proposals, however, leave a rather confusing and not entirely compatible mixture of individual, collective and state responses to housing and public administration and responsibility in the eventuality of the return. Likewise, although the conversion of the United States' military aid budget to Israel is envisaged as a probable financial source for the implementation of the return (leaving aside the fact that this supposition ignores the deeply problematic role the United States has played and plays in fuelling regional conflict), the significance and role, with the exception of UNRWA, of the international community and the governments hosting the refugee diaspora is ignored.

Sidelining the refugees' host states is particularly problematic for a number of reasons, not least of all because the right of return to Palestine-Israel could be responded to with the denial of the residency and citizenship rights, and in extreme circumstances the expulsion, of Palestinian individuals and/or communities who might wish to reclaim the right of return symbolically while remaining and settling in the country in which they were born in, or in a third state of their choice. Also, excluding the wider region from the frame of return is equally problematic in light of ongoing secondary and tertiary displacement of the Palestinian refugees from Syria (for more up-to-date information see report by the Palestinian Return Centre 2018). It is also surprising that the authors of the document fail to acknowledge that the return as envisioned potentially represents the biggest case of socially engineered mass movement, although there is precedent in the migrant absorption practiced by the State of Israel since its establishment, and for this reason the return might involve and require regional and international cooperation.

Nevertheless, despite the above well-intentioned critique, the aforementioned discrepancies and contradictions in the return vision document testify to the inclusion and inclusivity of a variety of voices and points of view in the process of thinking about the return. Likewise, the document represents a collaborative work in progress rather than a manifesto and calls forth further consideration and debate. The vision document also represents a radical reframing of the Palestinian return as the co-responsibility between the Israelis and Palestinians, and further demonstrates how Zochrot as an organization has grown and developed since its inception. This can be gauged in particular by contrasting the 2012 Cape Town Document co-authored by BADIL and Zochrot with the 2010 paper on the practicalities of return, published in a trilingual issue of the *Sedek* journal.

The paper 2010 paper entitled 'Thinking practically about the return of the Palestinian refugees' is co-authored by two of Zochrot's founders, Norma Musih and Eitan Bronstein. In this paper the framework underlying the thinking about the practicalities of the return is decidedly Jewish-Israeli-centric. The underlying assumption is that the decision-making process lies in the hands of Israelis: the Israeli public has to accept the return, it has to be assured of its safety and right to self-determination, and it will accommodate the absorption of the refugees into the existing body politic via a gradual process of return. Although, the 2010 paper similarly assumes a post-Zionist moment in which the return will take place, there is reluctance on the part of the Jewish-Israeli authors to see the Jewish-Israeli collectivity rearticulated otherwise and/or decolonized. What I mean by this is that there is an absence of an attempt to think beyond the dominant and prevailing logic of separation and segregation between Jewish-Israelis and Palestinians. For example, the post-return state is envisaged by the authors as a state comprised of numerous federal-type states, each responsible for its own governance and cultural management.

In contrast the 2012 vision document encourages bilingualism and calls for Arabic and Hebrew to be instituted as the official languages of the state which would have to be learnt by both collectivities, with emphasis on Jewish-Israelis learning Arabic as part of the decolonization process. The notion of Israelis as colonizers is also decidedly absent from the 2010 paper on the return, with a focus on righting the wrongs of 1948 without an acknowledgement that the Zionist project is an ongoing settler-colonial project both in the 1948 and 1967 territories. The Occupation is also curiously absent from the frame employed to examine the return. For example, the refugees in Lebanon are mentioned as deserving to be prioritized because their conditions are the worst. This is rather curious, given that the authors are writing four years after the imposition of the blockade on Gaza and in the aftermath of the 2008–9 attack, which is briefly mentioned in the paper in relation to future truth and reconciliation processes. Moreover, given that the majority of Gaza's residents are registered as refugees, one could argue that refugees from Gaza should be prioritized. This is not an attempt to create a hierarchy of refugees, which is highly problematic to begin with, but rather highlights the manner in which leaving out the Occupation from a framework which alludes to the possibility of a shared state by Jewish-Israelis and Palestinians can still reinforce the logic of separation which frames the contemporary settler-colonial regime.

Moreover, avoiding the subject of the Occupation is a means of avoiding responsibility in the present, or at least avoiding talking about taking the necessary action to bring about the post-Zionist state envisaged in the return documents: 'When I [we] remember, rewrite, retell the past, the new past turns my present into a narrative environment that becomes a type of norm, a constraining and enabling frame that defines what I [we] will need to oppose, celebrate, defy' (Rosello 2010: 18). Taking responsibility entails more than simple acknowledgement; it entails actions that would bring about some form of justice. It requires an urgent and serious working through the past or the undertaking of 'a practice and something between a politics and an ethics, something that could be called an agenda' (17). A renewed agenda which calls for practical solidarity in the present can create the necessary steps to redress the injustices of the past with view to creating a more just future.

There are many possibilities for what this agenda might look like. One possibility is a concerted focus not only on the acknowledgement of the Nakba but, more importantly, the recognition of the right of return within Israeli society. This is something that Zochrot activists have been working on since 2012 with two subsequent conferences on the return in 2013 and 2016. Yet while Zochrot activists accept the right of return as a given in both the 2010 paper and the 2012 vision document, nevertheless, it is not clear what the best means are to convince the Jewish-Israeli public to move away from the denial of the significance of the Nakba and the refusal to recognize the Palestinian right to redress.[6] The rise and retrenchment of right-wing nationalist politics across the world since around 2011 is an obstacle to any progressive and/or decolonial agenda for the foreseeable future. Despite their limitations and the sociopolitical obstacles they face, Israeli proponents of Nakba acknowledgement are carving out a vital space for dialogue within Israeli society which is increasingly enfolding in denial. This denial is most explicitly evident in the concerted political efforts to silence the Nakba narrative and intimidate its advocates. The significance of Zochrot's commemorative activities lies precisely in the act of bearing witness and the refusal to forget about the Nakba in a time of denial. Zochrot's remembrance activities are a reminder that denial and repression are not the same as forgetting, and, moreover, there is positive potential in the stand-off between those who seek to reconcile with the tragedy of the past and embrace a decolonial future and those who choose denial and conflict.

Conclusion

Since the 1990s the history of 1948 has been simultaneously read and reread as a historical account from the events of the past to the present, and in reverse, illuminating a silenced history and memory from the perspective of the now. Despite its catastrophic nature, the Nakba is also a narrative of hope, its narration having been made possible by the long-awaited recognition in the Oslo Accords of 1993 that the Palestinians are a national collectivity with rights to self-determination. The proliferation of Nakba testimonies and commemorations since the 1990s have been the direct result of the space, to re-narrate the Palestinian nation, opened up by the Oslo Accords with their promise of statehood. Narrating the Nakba became even more urgent when this promise, coupled with the refusal to address the refugees' right of return, began to appear as a distant and untenable prospect.

In response to these failures, the Palestinian collectivity and diaspora intellectuals, alongside a number of critical Israeli academics and civil society groups such as Zochrot, amongst others, have undertaken a project which seeks to challenge Israel's dominance over narrating the history of Palestine-Israel. Differential access to power has meant that who gets to tell the story of the Nakba with the biggest impact has not always been related to direct experience and its lived consequences, but the privilege of being able to speak and be received with authority, which at present tends to lie with Jewish-Israelis. Nevertheless, the conversation that is taking place between progressive Jewish-Israelis and Palestinians is vitally important as it is contributing to the production of new narratives for decolonial cohabitation.

3

Binationalism as settler decolonization? ICAHD and the One Democratic State

During the Israeli Committee Against House Demolitions (ICAHD) UK's 2010 annual conference in London, Jeff Halper, the founder of ICAHD, expressed regret for the use of the phrase 'redeeming' as opposed to 'decolonizing' in the subtitle of his semi-autobiographical political monograph *An Israeli in Palestine: Resisting Dispossession, Redeeming Israel* (2010). The original invocation of 'redemption' in the title of Halper's autobiography inadvertently draws on a key tenet in the Zionist settlement discourse with redemption referring to the Jewish return to Palestine and the transcendence of the diasporic exile (see Piterberg 2010). Thus, invoking redemption unwittingly reaffirmed Israel's settler-colonial project in Palestine. Halper's regret of the original linguistic omission and his subsequent substitution is exemplary of broader changes in consciousness among critical Jewish-Israeli civil society culminating in the adoption of the settler-colonial explanatory framework and the evolution of a decolonial discourse concerning Palestine-Israel's settler-colonial past and present, as well as her possible futures.

This chapter examines some of the emerging critical civil society debates in relation to the one-state solution being the most appropriate geopolitical arrangement for the articulation of freedom, justice and equality in Palestine-Israel. This is done with reference to ICAHD's 2012 statement in support of a binational state and the ensuing critiques it attracted from Palestinian supporters of the one-state position. Drawing on these debates which have largely revolved around Jewish-Israeli rights to political self-determination in Palestine-Israel, the chapter proposes that alternative versions of self-determination as cultural rights for the established Hebrew-speaking national community represent a more inclusive form of self-determination in the eventuality of decolonization. The chapter's key contribution to these ongoing debates is to suggest a rethinking of the relationship between the 'Jewish' and 'Israeli' components of the Jewish-Israeli identity, beginning with an acknowledgement of the role of 'Jewishness' in the Zionist settler-colonial project and its continuing deployment to justify Jewish diasporic settler colonialism, while denying the rights of return of the Palestinian refugee diaspora. Thus, a rearticulation of Jewish-Israeliness as a civic, cultural and linguistic community might better serve to break with settler-colonial privilege, while acknowledging and affirming the specificity and history of Hebrew cultural life in Palestine-Israel.

ICAHD: The Israeli Committee Against House Demolitions

ICAHD defines itself as a 'human rights and peace organization established in 1997 to end Israel's Occupation over the Palestinians. ICAHD takes as its main focus, as its vehicle for resistance, Israel's policy of demolishing Palestinian homes in the Occupied Palestinian Territory and within Israel proper. ICAHD was awarded ECOSOC Special Consultative Status in 2010' (ICAHD 2012a). The organization received the Olive Branch Award from Jewish Voice for Peace, USA; and Jeff Halper, ICAHD's co-founder and director, was nominated for the 2006 Nobel Peace Prize (ICAHD 2006). ICAHD's activities can be roughly summarized under four categories: (i) political analysis (reframing the conflict), (ii) practical solidarity (resisting demolitions and rebuilding), (iii) transnational advocacy (lobbying international governments and intergovernmental institutions) and (iv) alternative education tours (providing transnational activists with expert knowledge and information).

ICAHD's strong and vocal commitment to opposing the Occupation and standing side by side with Palestinians resisting house demolitions is respected and valued by Palestinian counterparts. Despite its name, the organization's activities are wide-ranging: from activists physically resisting house demolitions by getting in front of bulldozers, to providing legal advice and moral support to Palestinians seeking to apply for building permits, to challenging the Civil Administration's[1] negative rulings against Palestinian claimants, to taking the case against house demolitions to international legal institutions. Since 2011 the organization has expanded its activities to carry out legal research on the state of demolition practices within Israel as well as in the Occupied Territories, particularly focusing on demolitions of Bedouin villages in the Negev/Naqab. ICAHD's findings are regularly presented to international human rights committees in the European Union and United Nations. Moreover, ICAHD has sister organizations in the UK, the United States, Finland and Germany, with most members being seasoned Palestine solidarity campaigners, experienced at lobbying political representatives at the local, national and regional levels.

Unlike Zochrot which explicitly seeks to address Israeli society, ICAHD's role tends to be more focussed on grassroots solidarity with the Palestinian people, with an emphasis on international advocacy. Within Israeli society ICAHD's activities in the Occupied Territories and abroad are largely viewed as marginal, traitorous or obstructive (see NGO Monitor 2008). ICAHD's peace centre Beit Arabiya has been demolished several times by the Israeli army, often with explicit warnings. Similar to Zochrot, ICAHD's work and perspective have evolved alongside and as a result of constructive criticism levelled at them. This evolution in organizational narrative is most evident in the writing of Jeff Halper which oscillates between analysis and a call for action. When translated into action the obstacles posed by the situation on the ground make the biggest difference to enacting justice in practice. For example, solidarity with Gaza has become largely symbolic or humanitarian in nature because of Israel's long-standing blockade and restrictions on movement in and out of the territory.

Since 2011 ICAHD has made explicit links between house demolitions in the West Bank and house demolitions against Palestinian citizens of Israel within Israel's 1948 borders, bringing their thinking and work closer to a discourse of decolonization. However, lack of funds and the considerable higher cost of operating a construction site in Israel have prevented the organization from hosting an international rebuilding camp in the same way that they do on an annual basis in the West Bank. In recent years alongside its practical resistance activities in Palestine-Israel ICAHD has increasingly focussed on international advocacy, regularly briefing international politicians, decision makers and lawyers on the situation in the Occupied Territories. The year 2012 saw the launch of a new information pack including statistics on displacement trends, a legal briefing booklet on Israel's violation of international law as pertaining to house demolitions and displacements[2] specifically designed for international lawyers, as well as a detailed booklet containing political and normative analysis of Israel's displacement policies in the OPTs: 'Demolishing Homes, Demolishing Peace'.

Aside from the military occupation, corporate capital plays an equally significant role in many of the injustices suffered in Palestine-Israel. Corporate complicity is heavily intertwined and enmeshed in Israel's racialized regime of oppression and domination in the Occupied Territories, and to a lesser extent in Israel within the 1948 borders. As such, individual corporations are viewed as vehicles for and enablers of Israel's state interests and policies and as institutions which benefit directly and indirectly from the abuse and exploitation of the Palestinians (Winstanley and Barat 2011; Barghouti 2011; Wiles 2013). Despite differentiated emphasis on the role of state or corporate institutions as purveyors of injustice, the relationship between state and corporate institutions continues to shape the reality of Palestine-Israel. The policy of closure in the Occupied Territories which has barred and excluded most Palestinians from the Israeli employment market since the 1990s has resulted in an unemployment epidemic and growing impoverishment. At the same time many international and Israeli businesses particularly in the settlement blocks have benefitted and profited from Palestinian workers' desperation and the absence of a minimum wage and legal employment protection. In essence, profit accumulation has been shaped by racialized practices, and racialized policies have been enabled by a drive for profit accumulation which routinely disregards human rights (see also Clarno 2017).

Corporate complicity in Israel's Occupation of the West Bank and Gaza Strip has been particularly prominent in the physical infrastructure of the Occupation, from the several hundred international and Israeli companies involved in the construction, maintenance and surveillance of the Separation Wall, to Caterpillar's bespoke D9 armoured bulldozers used by the Israeli army in house demolitions and other destructive operations in the Occupied Territories (see Who Profits from the Occupation). A Caterpillar bulldozer was also infamously involved in the killing of US solidarity activist Rachael Corrie in 2003. On the whole, private companies play an essential role in the maintenance of the Occupation with many security services, including checkpoint management, having been subcontracted to private security firms such as G4S, with the company announcing its gradual divestment from Israel in 2016 (see Amrov 2016).

Corporate complicity in Israel's human rights abuses and violations has been the primary target of advocacy for boycott and divestment. ICAHD was one of the first Israeli groups to call for a boycott of the Israeli occupation, predating the 2005 Palestinian Civil Society call for BDS. ICAHD's original boycott statement included (i) an arms embargo on weapons sold to Israel for use in the Occupied Territories; (ii) boycott of settlement goods and businesses; (iii) trade sanctions against Israel for violating its EU agreement by labelling goods from the West Bank as 'Made in Israel'; (iv) divestment from corporations profiting from the Occupation; and (v) holding to account individuals, such as politicians and senior military personnel, responsible for human rights violations by trying them in international courts (ICAHD 2005). The organization's revised call for boycott in 2010 bought ICAHD under the framework of the Palestinian BDS call and expanded to include boycott of Israeli academic, cultural and sports institutions until they condemn the Occupation and disassociate themselves from it (see ICAHD 2021).

The binational statement

In September 2012, ICAHD, which had previously eschewed adopting a public position on a given state solution, issued a statement officially in support of a one-state solution. ICAHD, under the auspices of Jeff Halper, is in many respects one of the leading critical Israeli organizations that has spoken out on the subject of a one-state; though there are at present as many visions of a one-state as there are visionaries. Up until the publication of 'In the Name of Justice: Key Issues Around a Single State' (Halper and Epshtain 2012), Halper had been a strong proponent of what he refers to as a 'Regional Confederation', a concept inspired by the belief that Palestine-Israel is too small a unit to solve all of the key issues concerning the Palestinian refugees' right of return, water, trade, security, borders and population settlement. Instead, he advocated a regional set-up in which the Occupation of the 1967 territories would be dismantled, a viable and contiguous Palestinian state would be established on all of the 1967 territories, and a regional confederation, similar to the European Union, would emerge, comprising Palestine, Israel, Syria, Lebanon, Jordan and possibly Egypt, across which there would be free and unrestricted movement between the territories for the purposes of trade, settlement and visiting friends and relatives, and whereby the member states would collectively coordinate their security and environmental policy so as to ensure peace and the fair regional distribution of resources such as water (Halper 2012).

Despite a number of problematic assumptions underlying this proposal, it contributes two important arguments to the discussion on the nature of a possible solution to Palestine-Israel's predicament. Firstly, it underscores the idea that it is possible and desirable for Jewish-Israelis to cooperate with and integrate into the region as equal and valuable partners, thus debunking the security pretext for Israel's exceptionalist militarism. Secondly, it responds practically to the potential danger that an implementation of the right of return without regional cooperation can lead to the expulsion of those in the Palestinian refugee diaspora who might in fact wish to remain and settle in their host country rather than physically return to Palestine-Israel. In this respect, a regional confederation could ensure the security and human rights of both individuals and national collectivities in the region. However, underlying the federal proposal is reluctance about the possibility of a full implementation of the Palestinian refugees' right of return which may inevitably lead to the minoritarian status of Jewish-Israelis within Palestine-Israel and its myriad implications, notably the possibility for discrimination, oppression and expulsion. This is perhaps one of the key reasons why ICAHD's 2012 statement on a single state places great emphasis on a 'binational' government in Palestine-Israel, governance based on the principle of self-determination for Palestinians and Jewish-Israelis alike.

ICAHD's statement was welcomed by Palestinian counterparts for accepting Palestinian-Israeli cohabitation in a single state as a desirable resolution but was nevertheless criticized on key aspects. One of the prime contentions regarding Halper/ICAHD's formulation revolved around the right to national self-determination. Ali Abunimah – a prominent Palestinian diaspora activist, founder of *The Electronic Intifada*, an online publication for critical debate and discussion, and author of *One Country: A Bold Proposal to End the*

Israeli-Palestinian Impasse (2006) – criticized the ICAHD statement for its underlying implications of binationalism, which granted equal right of self-determination to the Jewish-Israeli settler collectivity as that of the displaced and colonized indigenous Palestinians (Abunimah 2012). Omar Barghouti (2012), another prominent Palestinian proponent of the one-state solution and a key figure in the BDS movement, also vocally rejected the application of the principle of self-determination to the Jewish collectivity in Palestine-Israel. He further emphasizes the fact that the Israeli state does not recognize 'Israeli' or even 'Jewish-Israeli' as a nationality. Under current Israeli law, only 'Jewish' is recognized as a nationality, therefore, privileging ongoing transnational Jewish extraterritorial claims to Palestine-Israel (also see Zreik 2008).

As part of his critique of the national question, Barghouti (2012) further cites two different international legal definitions pertaining to what constitutes a national collectivity, one of which is the 'Kirby definition', adopted by UNESCO, which stipulates that a people are 'a group of individual human beings who enjoy some or all of the following common features: history, ethnic identity, culture, language, territorial connection, etc.' (204). This definition is further extended to include that 'the group as a people must have the will to be identified as a people or the consciousness of being a people' (204). Barghouti then dismisses both of these definitions as currently inapplicable to Jewish-Israelis. In relation to the binational claim he further argues that 'bi-nationalism, initially espoused by liberal-Zionist intellectuals, is premised on a Jewish national right in Palestine, on par, and to be reconciled, with the national right of the indigenous, predominantly Arab population. Bi-nationalism today, despite its many variations, still upholds this ahistorical national right of colonial-settlers' (198).

While Barghouti is correct in asserting that binationalism is not a new or novel proposition, given that variants of it were advocated by Zionist and non-Zionist Jewish thinkers in the 1920s and 1930s (see Raz-Krakotzkin (2011) for a thorough critique of the inherent Orientalism in these early positions), there are nevertheless marked differences between contemporary one-state proposals and the positions supported by previous proponents of a geopolitical union in Palestine-Israel. These differences are largely due to the very different geopolitical reality being described and engaged with in the present. The original Jewish adherents to binationalism such as Gershom

Scholem, Martin Buber and the associated Brit Shalom group, among others, were partly advocating binationalism from a position of weakness. The Zionist settlement project was in its infancy, with Jewish settlement a minoritarian issue, and Palestine under British rule. The current reality is that the Zionist project to settle Palestine and establish a Jewish 'homeland', or at least Jewish domination in the land, has been achieved, and as such Jewish-Israeli proponents of binationalism are members of the dominant settler ethnonation in Palestine-Israel.

In other words, the binationalism of Brit Shalom was a binationalism of newcomers trying to establish a foothold in a coveted land. Contemporary Jewish-Israeli binationalists depart from this uncritical settlerist logic by conceding their right to exclusive possession of, and domination over, the land. The former can be characterized as a binationalism of settlers, while contemporary positions stem from a commitment to binationalism based on settler decolonization. This key difference is something that needs to be acknowledged and incorporated into Palestinian considerations of decolonization and cohabitation. Moreover, it is important to recognize and engage with the fact that the Israeli state's refusal to formalize an Israeli nationality,[3] which is perhaps one of the biggest obstacles to its decolonization and democratization, merely testifies to the extraterritorial schemes of the state rather than to a lack of identification among the Jewish-Israeli population as a people. For over seventy years, since 1948, Jewish-Israelis have shared and been defined by a common language and culture, namely Hebrew. They also share a common territorial identity corresponding to the 1948 borders, with the exception of post-1967 government settler-colonial designs, which have, for the most part, been disputed by a significant number of Israelis.

In addition, the most striking example of Jewish-Israeliness is embodied in the widespread willingness to be conscripted and serve in the Israeli Defence Forces. Even if one is to invoke the fact that many Israelis might speak another language or have family in another country, it would be similar to stating that US nationals, in spite of their settler-colonial past and present, multicultural and transnational origins, do not constitute a people with a perceived common identity as Americans. Therefore, even if one is to deny or refuse to accept national political self-determination to Jewish-Israelis in a shared future state on the basis of their settler-colonial origins, or to insist that they should see themselves as Palestinian Jews, as Uri Davis (2010) argues, it is nevertheless important to acknowledge and engage with the significance of existing national identifications among Israeli Jews in Palestine-Israel.

Abunimah's critique of ICAHD's one-state statement also raises some pertinent objections to the Jewish-Israeli right to ongoing and continued settlement in and domination over Palestine-Israel. His key argument is that as members of a settler-colonial nation, Jewish-Israelis are not entitled to collective self-determination the way that Palestinians are. This is because the historical-political context in which Jewish-Israeli nationalism emerged in Palestine-Israel has only been made possible because of the dispossession of the Palestinians. Therefore, Jewish-Israeli nationhood, which is settler-colonial and exogenous to Palestine, cannot claim self-determination in the manner that the Palestinians are entitled to by virtue of their indigeneity and their shared collective experience of political discrimination and dispossession.

Abunimah's argument that Jewish-Israelis are not entitled to a right to national political self-determination in Palestine-Israel on the basis that they are not indigenous and, moreover, that their constitution as a nation is based on dispossessive settler-colonialism, further raises the question of whether giving up the transnational diasporic Jewish right of return is a prerequisite for decolonization. Should Jewish return be suspended temporarily while the Palestinian refugee return is implemented? Or should the Law of Return[4] be suspended permanently? In fact, would the Jewish diaspora have a right to 'return' and consider Palestine-Israel as their 'national homeland' if decolonization succeeds? These questions require a consideration of the nature of Jewish-Israeliness, its relationship to Palestine-Israel, and the wider Jewish Diaspora, and consequently their right to national self-determination in Palestine-Israel. In many respects, these questions are fundamental to the process of decolonization, yet have no easy answers.

The necessity to rearticulate Jewish-Israeliness as non-dominating is at the centre of the possibility for decolonization. However, an emphasis on disavowal and self-negation is neither just nor practical for building co-resistance and working towards an egalitarian and just resolution to the ongoing settler colonization. For, as Leila Farsakh (2011) writes, presently 'the Palestinian debate on the one state solution, while inclusive of Jews, avoids engaging with the complexity of Jewish identity and history. It clearly repudiates Zionism, but it seeks to incorporate the Jewish person as a neutral repentant entity' (70). She calls on Palestinian advocates of the one-state solution to build alliances with critical anti-Zionist Israelis and to initiate and conduct

> an open discussion on identity and a free open space to understand Israeli culture in its Western dimensions as much as in its Arab roots which it often negates ... The second debate that needs to take place is about multiculturalism in Israel as well as in the Arab world and within Palestinian society, and how to reinvigorate the present Arab identity with the cosmopolitan character it once had. (Farsakh 2011: 70)

This is indeed a pertinent task that needs to be undertaken by critical scholars and activists, particularly in light of growing transnational post-nationalist interconnections across the Arab world and beyond. Sadly, the remainder of this chapter cannot do justice to this rich and complex topic. Rather, the primary concern here is to engage with contemporary rearticulations of Israeli Jewishness or Jewish-Israeliness in relation to the process of decolonization, seeking to raise a number of issues for further discussion and engagement. In this respect, the critical commentary that follows is not intended as a prescription for a future identitarian category, rather it is an attempt to articulate alternative formulations of Jewish-Israeli identification and the possibility for its decolonization.

My suggested reading of Jewish-Israeliness draws on a number of existing civil society alternatives to ICAHD's insistence on political Jewish self-determination in Palestine-Israel. These alternatives have in particular been articulated by activists working with Zochrot and, to a lesser extent, Anarchists Against the Wall (AATW). For the latter organization, decolonization is a process involving active resistance to, and the dismantling of, the apparatuses of occupation and colonization, while largely avoiding identitarian debates. However, this has led to accusations that participation by critical Jewish-Israelis in practical co-resistance activities reinforces a framing of anti-occupation activism as international solidarity activism in what is primarily a Palestinian national liberation struggle. Such reservations are, to a large extent, short-sighted and unwarranted, and both Marcelo Svirsky (2012, 2014a, 2014b) and Uri Gordon (2008) address them robustly in their work. Svirsky, in particular, sees co-resistance and the refusal to engage in identitarian politics as an articulative practice which attempts to bring about in the present new modes of cohabitation while working towards ultimate decolonization.

Zochrot activists similarly see decolonization as an internal process which has to take place within the Jewish-Israeli community, beginning with learning about and acknowledging that Palestinian dispossession is not only Palestinian history but also Jewish-Israeli history, and then working towards the implementation of the right of the Palestinian refugees to return. These attempts to conceptualize the Jewish-Israeli settler community in Palestine-Israel in terms of an established Hebrew-speaking national community provide a useful alternative conceptualization of Jewish-Israeli self-determination (Musih and Bronstein 2010). Their suggested form of self-determination in a shared state is sociocultural rather than geopolitical in nature and bears similarities to movements for cultural devolution in Europe, an example of this being Wales in the UK where Welsh national self-determination is embodied in the revival and practice of the Welsh language and cultural production, rather than a demand for ruling over a distinct ethnonational space. This model stands in contrast to the ethnonationalist co-governance model represented by Belgium which ICAHD's binational statement draws upon; a model which has been widely criticized for reinforcing the very ethnonational segregation it was meant to combat.

Reframing belonging

The above formulation requires further engagement with my chosen emphasis on identifying the settler collectivity as Jewish-Israeli and the significance of this strategy. While I subscribe to secular democratic principles of citizenship, the strategic use of this label is first and foremost an attempt to acknowledge the significance of identitarian politics in Palestine-Israel in the present, while attempting a critical examination and suggesting a possible reframing, which in turn calls for further consideration. With good intentions, many Palestinians and critical Israelis prefer to place emphasis on the 'Jewish' dimension as the redeemable ethno-religious category in a context of decolonization (for example, Uri Davis's 'Palestinian Jew', ICAHD's binational statement, the pre-Oslo PLO charter, etc.). From this perspective, the 'Israeli' component is considered to be imbued with the characteristics of Zionism and colonialism, and moreover implies acceptance of the Zionist settler-colonial project of the State of Israel, whereas the 'Jewish' harks back to an idealized vision of multi-denominational coexistence before the Zionist settler colonization of Palestine-Israel.

Both of these assumptions are deeply flawed and serve to reinforce Zionism's own logic of settler-colonial supremacy. Above all, Israel is not an 'Israeli' state, as Abunimah and Barghouti correctly point out: it is a Jewish-dominated state that happens to be called Israel. In fact, the Zionist settler-colonial project seeks exclusive ethno-religious transnational diasporic Jewish self-determination in Palestine-Israel (Zreik 2008) and the 2018 Nation State Law reinforces this analysis (see also Tatour 2019). Thus, treating the 'Jewish' component as the neutral term of the Jewish-Israeli dyad merely obscures the role played by the Zionist conceptualization of 'Jewishness' in its settler-colonial endeavour. One could argue, as Judith Butler (2012) does, that for this very reason Jewishness needs to be reclaimed from its Zionist conceptualization. As such, anyone interested in unpacking and challenging the Zionist policy of dispossession in Palestine-Israel needs to examine the role of Jewishness in this settler-colonial project in a critical and conscious manner, acknowledging the function of the concept in the Zionist project, without dismissing or denying the fact that Jewishness means many different things around the world and is experienced in many different ways by different people who have defined themselves as Jewish historically or contemporarily.

An emphasis on Jewishness, which also then results in debates over ethno-religious Jewish rights to self-determination in Palestine-Israel, implies that Jews everywhere in the world have the right to settle and claim collective rights in Palestine-Israel by virtue of being Jewish. The above notion of collective transnational Jewish self-determination in Palestine-Israel is the premise of Zionism and the practice of the State of Israel as it stands under the Law of Return. However, what needs to be considered is whether, in a decolonized and post-Zionist Palestine-Israel, in the twenty-first century, after decades of anti-colonial struggle across the world, a notion of transnational collective Jewish right in/over Palestine-Israel can still be justified. Furthermore, in full agreement with Abunimah and Barghouti on their insistence on a secular democratic formulation, conceptualizing rights in terms of ethno-religious and sectarian groupings is itself highly problematic and threatens to recreate a new version of segregation, perhaps akin to the set-up characterizing contemporary Lebanon, a set-up which contains the constant threat of inter-communal violence, something that a future decolonized Palestine-Israel would need to avoid.

Despite its violent and oppressive history, and the continuing violence, the notion of 'Jewish-Israeli' is also, arguably, the concept that best encapsulates, for the time being, the self-defined ethno/religious Jewish and/or Hebrew-speaking people who have lived in Palestine-Israel for the past 65–100 years. In that sense, 'Jewish-Israeli' or even 'Israeli', as a potentially secular category, could function in much the same way as the 'Afrikaner' identity functions in post-apartheid South Africa. Thus, although at present 'Israeli' carries the connotation of violence and dispossession by association with belonging to the Israeli settler-colonial state, in a post-colonial situation it has the potential of becoming a cultural and not a political signifier. Over time, Israeli Jewishness has the potential of being rearticulated as a civic identity, allowing for Jewishness to be reclaimed as an ethno-religious and/or cultural self-identification rather than the racialized category it signifies in the current settler-colonial State of Israel. It also helps to avert the rather problematic attempt by some to reduce Jewishness to religion and religious practice, an attempt which denies the significance of the multiple ways in which Jewish self-identification has developed over the past two centuries.

In addition to drawing attention to the need to unpack and engage with the inherent tension between the 'Jewish' and 'Israeli' components in contemporary Jewish-Israeli identification and its potential for decolonization, the above formulation also requires further engagement with another significant aspect in relation to Palestine-Israel. Namely, the diasporic and/or transnational nature of the two national collectivities, which further complicates questions of self-determination within Palestine-Israel, not least because both populations can claim belonging, even if not indigeneity. To begin with, it is paramount that some of the more unique aspects and particularities of the Palestine-Israel situation be acknowledged in order to examine possibilities for decolonization in a way that is constructive and involves the least amount of symbolic and/or real violence towards the indigenous and established settler communities in Palestine-Israel.

Palestine-Israel is not only a state created and settled by a transnational population with claims to diasporic origins in Palestine-Israel (see Sand (2009) for a critical perspective on the origins of the Jewish diaspora), but, moreover, the creation of the Jewish settler-colonial state, in the process of expelling the majority of the indigenous Palestinian population in 1948, has in turn resulted in the birth of one of the largest diasporas in the world. Currently, nearly half of all Palestinians live in the diaspora, with many never having been allowed to visit and/or return to Palestine-Israel and might not be permitted to do so in their lifetime. This makes the geopolitical dimensions of the conflict and any rights-based claims transnational and extraterritorial in a way that is not comparable to any other contemporary situation. For this reason, claims and counterclaims to indigeneity and exogeneity, justice in, and rights in and to the land of Palestine-Israel need to be carefully unpacked and considered in relation to actual and lived realities as well as aspirations for a just future.

An appeal to an inclusive politics of belonging can perhaps offer a better solution to the problem of securing decolonial cohabitation between settled Jewish-Israelis and the Palestinians. An inclusive politics of belonging would build on the notion of 'belonging' as defined by embodied spatial and geopolitical configurations (Trudeau 2006) and individuals' and groups' location in relation to and in association with others who are similarly located (Carrillo Rowe 2005). As Probyn (1996: 19) argues, belonging, as opposed to identity, 'captures more accurately the desire for some sort of attachment, be it to other people, places, or modes of being, and ways in which individuals and groups are caught within wanting to belong, wanting to become, a process that is fuelled by yearning rather than a position of identity as a stable state'. Such a notion highlights the centrality and potential of building on a shared attachment to place, and the identification of the geographical space of Palestine-Israel as 'home' for both the indigenous and settler collectivities.

While the politics of belonging presupposes a notion of belonging as emotional attachment to place, belonging and the politics of belonging are nevertheless two separate but related concepts (Antonsich 2010). Drawing on the work of Yuval-Davis (2006, 2011) this chapter calls for the need to articulate an inclusive politics of belonging that goes beyond legalistic and ethnocentric interpretations of the right to self-determination, and seeks instead to centre the notion of 'home' as opposed to 'homeland' in thinking through decolonial cohabitation. What I mean by this is that there is a need to consider established Jewish-Israeli settlers as belonging in Palestine-Israel by virtue of their sense of emotional attachment to the place, and therefore as having the right to actualize themselves as individuals and as a cultural collectivity in a decolonial and non-dominating way. This type of an inclusive politics of belonging equally applies to the right to belong for non-colonial migrant settlers, echoing the sentiment of No One Is Illegal that 'everyone who is here belongs here' (see Walia 2013), such an understanding of belonging requires a commitment to decolonial forms of association and cohabitation that reject domination and oppression.

Thus, while Abunimah (2010, 2012) is correct in arguing that in the present the principle of self-determination only applies to indigenous and/or minority ethnic groups, nevertheless some form of acknowledgement of collective identification among Jewish-Israelis has to take place given the long history of conflict and the undeniable presence of two national groups which are strongly defined and established along ethnonational lines, at least at the present time. An acknowledgement of, and a more concerted critical engagement with, the rights claims of Jewish-Israelis would further serve to alleviate the fears of expulsion in the eventuality of decolonization, fears also shared by some critical Israelis. An example of this is Halper's (2013) response to Abunimah and Barghouti's critique of ICAHD's 2012 binational proposal where he argues that the position that Jewish-Israelis have no right to self-determination in Palestine-Israel,

> shared though not usually articulated so clearly by many of the Palestinian Left, begins to resemble the position of Hamas (or, inversely, the settlers), based though it is on anticolonial indigenous rights rather than religion. It leaves unclear the civil status of Israelis/ Jews in this one democratic but not bi-national state. At best, this would lead to an ethnocracy comparable to Israel today, with Israeli Jews possessing the unacceptable civil status suffered by 'Israeli Arabs' today. Or it might take the form of Zimbabwe, where a European minority was allowed to stay but ended up with limited civil rights, or even an Algeria where the French settler colonialists were forced to leave immediately upon liberation. In short, crucial issues of collective rights in a single state have been left deliberately vague.

Although the above sentiment can be critiqued for misreading Abunimah and Barghouti's rejection of Jewish self-determination as primarily a rejection of an extraterritorial Jewish right to settler colonization of Palestine-Israel, it is nevertheless not only a call for an acknowledgement of Jewish-Israeli identity but more so a request for affirmation of the right to remain and culturally self-determine in the process of decolonization. An acknowledgement of this concern can further serve to encourage currently inactive Jewish-Israelis to join and play an active part in the struggle for decolonization. Though, naturally, egalitarian and democratic cohabitation would require that in the long-run nationalistic identifications gradually yield to other more civic minded forms of belonging.

Conversely, as an acknowledgement of the historical and ongoing injustice perpetrated against the Palestinians, decolonization in Palestine-Israel would require an end to geopolitical claims to self-determination in Palestine-Israel by transnational Jewish communities. The return to the homeland being the prerogative of the Palestinian refugee diaspora, while non-Israeli Jewish individuals and communities who might wish to migrate to Palestine-Israel would become subject to open and fair migration procedures in the same way as all other exogenous individuals and collectivities wishing to reside in Palestine-Israel (Yiftachel (2010) makes a similar proposal). Therefore, an end to a transnational right to Jewish settlerism in Palestine-Israel must accompany the geopolitical and psychosocial decolonization of the land and its people, allowing for the indigenous and established settler communities to formulate and articulate new forms of cohabitation and identification.

The One Democratic State Campaign

Since 2018 a group of Jewish-Israelis and Palestinians have initiated the One Democratic State Campaign, a self-defined 'Palestinian-led' initiative which seeks to mainstream the notion of a single state. Jeff Halper is among the campaign's signatories and continues to make a key contribution to its theoretical development. The campaign has clearly integrated a settler-colonial analysis as the redemptive sociopolitical framework which would allow Palestinians and Jewish-Israelis to work towards decolonization and cohabitation. The 'apartheid' label, nevertheless, continues to be used strategically as a 'warning' of what may come if the colonial situation remains and intensifies through Israel's formal annexation of the West Bank. The campaign has produced a short manifesto which outlines a vision for the one democratic state, and there are plans to produce a constitution for the state which will be modelled on the ANC constitution which was written before the formal end of apartheid and adopted by the post-apartheid government in South Africa. The campaign's manifesto affirms the right of return, a commitment to non-discrimination, and a refusal to privilege any one given community over another. Taking into account the religious character of the constituent populations, the campaign avoids explicit calls for secularism although the proposed state itself will be non-denominational. At present the campaign has a small number of signatories. However, it is a step in the right direction in terms of an explicit call to build a Palestinian-led coalition which would work towards explicit advocacy for a one-state solution. If adopted by the BDS movement, such an initiative may gather rapid momentum. Although it is worth noting that the campaign does not have explicit links to the BDS movement at present.

Conclusion

The above considerations of Jewish-Israeli identification in relation to belonging, binationalism and self-determination in Palestine-Israel acknowledge the validity of ICAHD's binational position, in as far as it is a recognition of the recurrent ethnocentric set-up in Palestine-Israel. In light of criticisms from Palestinian counterparts, when examined from the perspective of the all-affected, particularly taking into account the rights of the dispossessed and disenfranchised Palestinian Diaspora, Jewish political self-determination in a decolonized Palestine-Israel appears unjust and deeply problematic. However, an alternative to ICAHD's binationalism is offered in the conceptualization of binational cohabitation as cultural self-determination. The unprecedented convergence between critical Palestinian and Israeli thought in relation to the necessity to rearticulate the situation in Palestine-Israel as one of settler-colonialism and to work towards the possibility for decolonization is the by-product of the failures of the official peace process. While the resulting advocacy for cohabitation in a single democratic state, signalling a move away from the discourse of ethnonational separation embodied in the two-state solution paradigm, is to be welcomed, it is, nevertheless, important to remain cautiously optimistic. At present, the role played by critical Israeli groups such as Zochrot, AATW and ICAHD, in terms of challenging the dominant framing of Zionist settler colonialism, is significant but remains a minority position both within the transnational movement for justice in Palestine-Israel and within Jewish-Israeli society.

What these groups highlight is not only the possibility for critical engagement and convergence between Palestinian and Jewish-Israeli interests towards peaceful cohabitation, but also the necessity to expand the terrain for contestation and engagement with and within Jewish-Israeli society. As such, critical responses by Palestinian counterparts must address the anxieties expressed and felt by many Israelis in relation to the possibility of decolonization. The question raised by ICAHD's binational statement and Halper's subsequent response to Palestinian criticisms is primarily a request for reassurance that there will be a place for Jewish-Israelis in a decolonized Palestine-Israel. This is perhaps something the BDS movement, particularly its Palestinian leadership, might wish to address. The ANC strategy of reaching out to the Afrikaner community during the anti-apartheid struggle might be a place to draw inspiration from. Alternatives are also present in similar situations such as Aotearoa New Zealand (see Bell 2009). However, at the same time it is important for critical Israelis to remain cognizant of the privileged and relatively powerful position in which their identity has been constructed to date, the necessary deconstruction of which is a precondition for decolonization.

The above considerations seek to highlight the importance of acknowledging and thinking through questions of identity and belonging as part of the cultural and symbolic process of decolonization. This analysis is underpinned by an intersectional framework which foregrounds cohabitation/reconciliation as a relation of justice and a commitment to justice which necessitates a critical reframing and rearticulation of the classed, gendered and racialized structures which maintain settler colonialism and the injustice it represents. Such a critical approach is necessary, not only in thinking about a just solution to Palestinian and Jewish-Israeli cohabitation but also in thinking beyond the binational binary, and moving to address the needs of all citizens irrespective of their ethnonational affiliations. In the words of Harsha Walia (2013: 249):

> Decolonisation is more than a struggle against power and control; it is also the imagining and generating of alternative institutions and relations ... [It] requires a fundamental reorientation of ourselves, our movements, and our communities to think and act with intentionality, creativity, militancy, humility, and above all, a deep sense of responsibility and reciprocity.

4

Vulnerability as a politics of decolonial solidarity: The case of the Anarchists Against the Wall

For over seventy years the Palestinians have been a stateless nation and Palestine has been absent from the maps of the world. Since 29 November 1947 when the international community voted for UN General Assembly Resolution 181 (II), which proposed the partition of Palestine into a Jewish state (52 per cent) and an Arab state (48 per cent), the land of Palestine became a golden map worn on a chain around the necks of Palestinian refugees (see Sa'di 2008). The dispossession of the indigenous population of Palestine as a national community was completed in the aftermath of the 1948 War when the State of Israel was established as sovereign and independent on 78 per cent of the former land of Palestine. The remaining 22 per cent of the Palestinian populated territories of the Gaza Strip and West Bank came under Egyptian and Jordanian control respectively until Israel came to militarily occupy both territories in 1967. The Occupation of the Gaza Strip and West Bank remains in effect at the time of writing.

Rashid Khalidi (1997) designates the First Intifada in 1987, or the popular Palestinian uprising against Israel's Occupation, as the catalyst for Israel's recognition of the Palestinians as a legitimate political counterpart which resulted in the signing of the Oslo Accords in 1993–5. The Second Intifada, on the other hand, is often rendered as the reason for the termination of the US-sponsored Oslo peace process (see Khalidi 2006). However, such an analysis ignores the evidence which suggests that in many respects the Second Intifada was a consequence of the ongoing Occupation, the brutal repression of the First Intifada, and the failures of the Oslo peace process. Moreover, the Oslo period created and consolidated Palestinian economic dependence on

Israel and witnessed the beginning of the policy of 'closure': partially, then permanently blocking Palestinian entry from the Occupied Territories to Israel, a situation exasperated by the fragmentation of the West Bank into administrative zones A, B and C (Haddad 2016; Hever 2010; Klein 2007; Turner 2015).

Even before the outbreak of the Intifada, most of the evidence points to the fact that there would be no implementation of UN resolution 242 (1967) or 338 (1973), both of which call for an end to the Occupation. Although many consider the Oslo Accords to be the blueprint for a two-state solution, there is no mention of the establishment of a Palestinian state either in the Declaration of Principles or the subsequent Interim Agreement. On the contrary, both Accords are very explicit that the final status issues pertaining to statehood and sovereignty, such as borders, settlements and refugees, remain outstanding. Article V.1 of the 1993 Declaration of Principles, or Oslo I, established a framework for an interim period of five years which would lead to Israel's full withdrawal from the Gaza Strip and West Bank. Article VII.5 of the Accord also called for the creation of a Palestinian Council, also known as the Palestinian Authority (PA), which would take over from the Civil Administration, Israel's military government in the Occupied Territories. The Accord specified that Israel had to provide a schedule for withdrawal within a year of the Declaration of Principles coming into effect in September 1993.

The second Oslo Accord, known as the Interim Agreement 1995, resulted in the establishment of the PA and the transfer under its control of major towns and cities including Bethlehem, Hebron, Nablus, Tulqarem and Ramallah, alongside a further 450 villages. In addition, the Accords carved up the Occupied Territories into Areas A, B and C. The PA's jurisdiction, also known as Area A, together with Area B, where the PA has 'joined' responsibility for civilian affairs, but not security, constitutes fewer than 28 per cent of the West Bank. During the Oslo Interim Period between 1994 and 1999 Israel doubled its settler population in the West Bank (Foundation for Middle East Peace 2012; Levinson 2009). During the same period the settler population in the Gaza Strip also increased but at a far lower rate. Simultaneously, the occupying state subjected the Palestinian population under its military rule in Area C of the West Bank to discriminatory policies of land expropriation and house demolitions (see Abu Zahra 2007; Hammami 2016).

By the outbreak of the Intifada in 2000 it was relatively clear that Israel had little intention of meeting the minimum requirements for withdrawal set out in the 1993 Declaration of Principles resulting in the failure of the Camp David negotiations. The ensuing Palestinian uprising provided the Israeli right-wing with a pretext to begin constructing the proposed 712 km long West Bank barrier. At the time of writing, 65 per cent of the construction has been completed and approximately 85 per cent of this is built on West Bank land (see OCHAOPT 2018). Despite its representation as a violent uprising, the Second Intifada utilized many of the same tactics of non-violent civil disobedience as those used during the First, including breaking military curfews and boycotting Israeli goods and businesses (Qumsiyeh 2010; Darweish and Rigby 2015). Albeit, the effectiveness of coordinated mass civil disobedience in the Second Intifada was drastically reduced with Israel's policy of border closure (see Klein 2007; Weizman 2007), the heavily restricted movement between the Gaza Strip and West Bank, and the annexation of East Jerusalem (see Abu Zahra 2007; Hanafi 2009).

The struggle against the Wall

A flagship example of the continuity and persistence of non-violent popular resistance post-Oslo and in the aftermath of the Second Intifada is the story of the two-decade-long protests against the Separation Wall in the West Bank. The beginning of the construction of the West Bank Separation Wall gave birth to the popular Palestinian committees of the Stop the Wall Campaign (see Carter Hallward and Norman 2011; Norman 2010; Qumsiyeh 2010; Darweish and Rigby 2015) which at the time of writing continue to organize and hold weekly non-violent demonstrations against land confiscations and the construction of the Separation Wall. The weekly Friday protests have resulted in some legal gains. In light of the International Court of Justice's ruling in 2004 on the illegality of the Wall's construction beyond the Green Line, legal petitions to the Israeli High Court were filed and led to the rerouting of the Wall away from some village lands (see Sfard 2018). However, escalating violent repression by the Israeli military has meant that other villages have not been able to translate protest into legal success.

The Second Intifada also ushered in the unprecedented involvement of international solidarity activists, and the formation of the International Solidarity Movement (ISM) in 2001. Palestinian activists established the ISM to encourage internationals from some of the most privileged states in the world, primarily from North America and Europe, to go to the Occupied Territories and take part in accompaniment activities. The purpose of these activists was to use their privileged international status to shield Palestinian activists and civilians targeted with excessive Israeli military violence, to break military-imposed curfews and bring food to besieged localities, as well as to advocate for Palestinian rights abroad and bear witness to the Palestinian struggle upon their return home (Clark 2009; Dudouet 2009; Schwietzer 2009).

Since its inception in 2001, ISM has attracted hundreds of international activists, a quarter of which are estimated to have Jewish heritage (Seitz 2003). Its activities, reflections from activists and media reports about the group have been highly publicized and are the subject of *Peace Under Fire*, edited by Josie Sandercock (2004). The ISM has also been embroiled in a number of international controversies, including the killings of two of its activists by Israeli soldiers in the Gaza Strip on two separate occasions. Subsequent Israeli military raids of the organization and a crack down on its associated activists, many of who were deported and barred from entering Israel and de facto the Occupied Territories, has meant that the organization has since around 2005 operated on a much smaller scale (Gordon 2010). The personal sacrifices made by ISM activists and Israel's violent responses to the organization has meant that ISM has achieved a significant level of respect among Palestinian and other international solidarity organizations, and activism under the rubric of ISM continues to play a significant role in international solidarity against the Wall.

In 2003, during a protest camp held in the village of Mas'ha which was jointly set up by Palestinian, Israeli and international activists on the proposed route of the West Bank Separation Wall, another direct-action group came into being: 'Anarchists Against the Wall' (AATW) who gained media publicity in the aftermath of a solidarity action during which an Israeli soldier shot and wounded one of the Israeli activists. Gordon and Grietzer (2013) define the Mas'ha camp as a moment which provided Israeli activists with an opportunity to differentiate themselves from the ISM and to make the presence of Israeli activists more visible and prominent within the protest. Pallister-Wilkins (2009) adds to this origin story anecdotal evidence that the Israelis were 'shamed' into publicizing their presence given the much higher visibility and greater presence of internationals in solidarity with the Palestinian struggle against the Wall. Hammami (2016) similarly notes that while Israeli activists are present at demonstrations and political actions, Palestinians often see internationals as the more committed party because they tend to live with the communities they are co-resisting with.

The anarchists were not the first Israeli group to be involved in direct action in the Occupied Territories. In fact, both AATW and ISM were predated by the joint Arab-Israeli grassroots group Ta'ayush, 'partnership' in Arabic (see Shulman 2007), with members of Ta'ayush being actively involved in setting up ISM and subsequently becoming active in AATW (Gordon 2010). However, although Israeli anti-occupation activism has a long history and predates the presence of significant numbers of international solidarity activists, the Israeli-Palestinian activist relationship is also much more complicated. Israelis are not strangers from abroad who come to act in solidarity with an oppressed group. They are in fact members and citizens of the settler-colonial collective which is responsible for and directly benefits from the colonization and dispossession of the Palestinians (for a more in-depth analysis of the related and even more complicated role and anti-Occupation activism of the Jewish diaspora see Stamatopoulou-Robbins 2008). For this reason, Israeli activists have been keen to disassociate themselves from both the 'international' and 'solidarity' labels and to emphasize their role as radical, critical and, more recently, decolonial Israelis. 'Joint' or 'collaborative' struggle have become the preferred terms for Israelis engaged in protests against the Wall (Gordon 2010; Svirsky 2014a, 2014b).

The emphasis on decolonization and joint struggle have been the direct result of the adoption of the settler-colonial framework into activist praxis. This evolving praxis is greatly indebted to activist-scholar participation in and reflection on the first decade of co-resistance against the Separation Wall (see Ronnie Barkan in Dalla Negra 2012; Gordon and Grietzer 2013; Gordon 2016; Svirsky 2014a, 2014b; Weizman 2017). This chapter's contribution to this ongoing conversation is to theorize the ways in which the widespread adoption of the settler-colonial framework by Israeli and international solidarity activists active in the non-violent struggle against the West Bank Separation Wall has contributed to the evolution of a praxis of decolonial solidarity articulated through the strategic mobilization of vulnerability vis-à-vis the violence, repression and dispossession of the settler-colonial state.

Mobilizing vulnerability as a politics of decolonial solidarity

From the onset of the non-violent struggle against the Wall, as an acknowledgement of their privileged structural position, the Israeli anarchists have been keen to stress that their role is primarily one of providing on-the-ground support to a struggle that is led first and foremost by those who it affects, namely the Palestinian residents of the villages along the Wall's route (see Barkan in Dalla Negra 2012; Snitz 2004, 2013). Moreover, at least during the early years of the struggle, AATW activists felt that their presence as privileged Israeli citizens provided some form of protection against unchecked Israeli military violence and the likelihood of the army using live ammunition on the protesters. As one anarchist activist explains:

> We believe that a nonviolent struggle puts more pressure on the Israelis. When the army has to deal with civilians, it has to bring in a far larger number of soldiers. They can't open fire at them freely, at least we hope not. In spite of the best efforts of organizers, almost every week of demonstrations ends with at least a few wounded. 262 people have been injured and 5 killed in the village of Bidu, near Jerusalem. One of these killed was a boy of 11. (Ayalon 2004: 11)

Gordon and Perugini (2016: 169) refer to the above praxis as 'a politics of human shielding' which mobilizes 'a politics of vulnerability' as a tool of protection against state violence. Butler (2016) similarly theorizes the role of vulnerability in non-violent resistance to state violence as 'a deliberate mobilization of bodily exposure'. In the above case of privileged lives acting in concert with the colonized in resistance, the mobilization of bodily vulnerability articulates a politics of decolonial solidarity. This articulation, however, remains embroiled in unequal power and status differentials, for not everyone who assembles to protest or take part in political action experiences vulnerability in the same way.

Vulnerability is not the same as precarity; even though precarity presupposes vulnerability (Butler 2016). The latter being the consequence of a strategy of power which involves deliberately exposing certain lives to harm, poverty and insecurity by denying them the necessary political, social and economic infrastructures to sustain their life and livelihood prior to any act of mobilization (Butler 2004, 2015, 2016). In the face of precarity, the very survival and continued existence of racialized populations subjected to violence and violation can be viewed as resistance against dispossessive and genocidal power (see also Weheliye 2014). The notion of 'existence as resistance' has a long history in the slogans of many indigenous and black resistance movements in North America, Palestine and elsewhere (see Butler 2016; Estes 2019; Taylor 2016). Political mobilization as an embodied enactment, however, goes beyond precarious existence as a form of resistance. Political mobilization serves to overcome vulnerability in the face of precarity through deliberate exposure to state violence. In that sense, the mobilization of vulnerability as a strategy of resistance is agentic in a way that surviving precarity is not.

The strategic mobilization of vulnerability has been at the core of Palestinian activist resistance to the settler-colonial strategy of dehumanization, devaluation and neglect to the point of death of the colonized Palestinian population (see Ghanim 2008; Hammami 2016). Settler-colonial state violence has been and continues to be one of the key strategies for the subjugation and elimination of Palestinian indigenous sovereignty (see Ghanim 2008; Hammami 2016; Mbembe 2003; Moreton-Robinson 2015; Wolfe 2006, 2016a). This violence is continuously justified in the name of protecting and securing the Jewish-Israeli settler collectivity from the Palestinian 'threat' (see Abdo 2014; Abdo and Lentin 2004 Abdo and Yuval-Davis 1995; Butler 2004, 2009). The strategic mobilization of vulnerability as a politics of decolonial solidarity, therefore, stands in stark contrast to the settler-colonial state's mobilization of vulnerability in the name of a politics of securitization (see also Butler 2009, 2016).

The story of the Wall tends to narrate the conflict from the Second Intifada, characterizing Palestinian actions as a rejection of peace (see Beilin 2006).

From this perspective the Wall's proclaimed purpose is to protect Israel from 'hostile penetration' by Palestinian terrorists. Perversely, the fear of terrorism appears not to prevent continuing illegal Jewish-Israeli settlement beyond the Green Line. Nor does it explain why the route of the Wall snakes into Palestinian territory and incorporates large blocks of the illegal settlements into Israel proper (see Eldar and Zertal 2007). This strategy represents an irreconcilable paradox whereby the settler-colonial state insists on barricading itself against danger and undesirable aspects of coexistence even as it aspires to greater sovereignty.

Moreover, the Israeli state's self-projection as vulnerable is a glaring example of Israel's desire to disavow its own ongoing responsibility for and actual perpetration of violence against the Palestinians. The Wall conceals over five decades of military occupation even as it reinforces it. It seeks to keep Palestinians out of Israel while constantly increasing the number of Jewish-Israeli settlers on the other side of the Wall, making them potentially vulnerable to the very violence the state claims it wishes to protect its citizens from (see also Eldar and Zertal 2007). In short, even as the Wall claims to protect from the blowback of the Occupation, it is itself a tool of the Occupation, the very construction of which demands the perpetration of structural and physical violence, whether through expropriating land and destroying the homes of Palestinians who happen to live on the proposed route of the Wall (see Ghanim 2008) or by violently suppressing popular protest, as in the villages of Bil'in, Budrus, Nabih Saleh, Ni'lin and others (see Burnat and Davidi 2011; also Snitz 2013).

From the perspective of the privileged citizen, that is, those who confer power onto the state and expect protection from danger in return, the desire for walling is not just about shoring up the border against external threat. It is a psychological act of expelling the perpetration of violence against others. This desire articulates itself as the wish to see oneself as 'good', 'innocent' and 'pure', while projecting characteristics of danger and violence onto the excluded Other (see Brown 2010; Butler 2004). In this context, the only basis on which co-resistance and co-operation between the indigenous and settlers who want to decolonize can take place is through taking part in vulnerability-based decolonial solidarity. By acting in concert with the colonized-in-resistance racially privileged settler-activists can serve to subvert and unsettle the settler-colonial normative-framing which legitimizes state violence in the name of protecting settler citizens from the threat of the indigenous demand for decolonization.

The paradox of decolonial solidarity

As Jawad argues a 'central performance strategy of the Bil'in Friday demonstrations [against the Wall] is thus making visible how the resistance to violence is continually met with violence' (2011: 137). Consequently, the presence of Jewish-Israelis resisting colonial land expropriation side by side with Palestinians directly challenges the representation of the Palestinians as an existential threat to Jewish-Israelis and shines a light on the violent nature of the settler-colonial state. Moreover, shared experiences of colonial violence during protest actions have played a central role in unsettling notions of settler privilege among Israeli activists. In the process, previously unthinkable decolonial affinities between Jewish-Israeli and Palestinian activists have been created and strengthened. The above assertion is illustrated by the story told by AATW activist Chen Misgav about one Friday afternoon when gas canisters 'rained' on gathering protesters before the planned start of the demonstration in Nabi Saleh, widely considered to be one of the villages which has faced the most violence from the Israeli army. As the army fires tear gas at the protesters, the activists are forced to run for cover and end up bursting through the door of an unknown Palestinian woman who immediately gave them raw onions to help with the effects of the gas:

> It wasn't my first visit to a Palestinian home, but it was certainly the first time in which I burst into a house whose owner I didn't know. The physical experience and the fear of what was going on outside were shared by all of us, Palestinians and Jewish Israelis, and to a large extent, eased the differences between us. The borders placed between us were crossed within a few minutes of the start of the demonstration. But other borders were also crossed – borders between public and private spaces, between home and outside, and between safe and dangerous places. For the first time in my life I felt safer in a Palestinian home than outside with soldiers from the very army I had served in. (Misgav 2013: 133)

The shared vulnerability to violent assault, facing arrest, injury, or even the possibility of death, helps to create bonds and understanding that go beyond mere rhetoric. As well as crossing real and metaphorical borders of enmity, the vulnerability-based decolonial solidarity of AATW also helps to create relations between Palestinians and Jewish-Israelis that are based on mutuality and solidarity, articulating an Israeli Jewishness as decolonial and non-dominating (also see Turner 2015; Weizman 2017). This in turn signals the possibility for cohabitation which is not based on the violent and dispossessive hierarchies of the settler-colonial logic. Writing about the arrest of Jonathan Pollak, the Palestinian activist Ayed Morrar (2010: n.p.) reasserts the centrality of decolonial solidarity in co-resistance against the Wall as he reflects on the emerging and sustained moments of identification between Palestinians and Israelis during protest actions:

> Jonathan Pollak is a friend whose friendship I am proud to share … I wouldn't dare to build a friendship with an Israeli outside of resistance to the occupation, because of how the occupation distorts the meanings of human relationships, and because dignity would not allow me to have a relationship with someone who feels superior to me because of their power, gender, religion or ethnicity. Jonathan Pollak is a man trying to prove that those who believe in occupation cannot claim to be humanitarian or civilized. He also wants to prove that resisting oppression and occupation does not mean being a terrorist or killing. This freedom fighter, Jonathan Pollak, leaves a prison cell only to be sentenced again by the Israeli occupation authorities, and recovers from one of his solidarity demonstrations only to be injured again in the next one.

The decolonial identification and solidarity which has emerged over the past two decades of co-resistance against the Wall as a result of the willingness to put one's body on the line is something that has earned a great deal of respect for the anarchist activists. However, as Rema Hammami (2016) reminds us, writing on the related subject of international and Israeli accompaniment of Palestinian communities targeted for ethnic cleansing in Area C of the West Bank, the successful mobilization of vulnerability in the service of non-violent resistance relies on Palestinian communities and activists building solidarities with 'bodies that count' (see also Hyndman 2005). The politics of creating alliances with bodies that count are of course highly problematic as they inadvertently reproduce the very colonial hierarchies of life that they seek to subvert and resist (see also Mahrouse 2014). Furthermore, instances of state violence against racially privileged lives are incredibly rare and continue to be characterized by the settler-colonial economy of life which privileges certain lives at the expense of the devaluation and destruction of others.

The operation of the unequal valuation of life was evident in the cases of Rachel Corrie and Tom Hurndall, two ISM activists who were killed in Gaza in the early 2000s, and which subsequently received a great deal of international media coverage. The Palestinians they stood in solidarity with, on the other hand, are often represented as faceless brown bodies who only count when there is a high body count (see Butler 2009; Ghanim 2008; Hammami 2016). Similarly, Israel's liberal media interest in the protests against the Wall in the aftermath of the shooting and near-fatal wounding of the Israeli activist Gil Na'amati by Israeli soldiers in 2003 can be sharply contrasted with the complete lack of media coverage of the many dozens of Palestinian protestors killed or wounded since the start of the protests. In the rare instances when Israeli or international solidarity activists are targeted with colonial state violence they are constituted as 'bodies out of place' (Hammami 2016: 185), marked out by their deviance and 'rendered precarious by aligning [themselves] with a political enemy' (Amir and Kotef 2014: 679). Simultaneously, the potential 'woundability', and even 'killability', of Israeli activists serves an important purpose as it signals a break from the Israeli Zionist hegemony and constitutes a symbolic and corporeal convergence with the Palestinian struggle for decolonization (also see Amir and Kotef 2014; Weizman 2017). This in turn can give rise to the emergence of new articulations of resistance to colonization, and ultimately to decolonization.

Presently, however, there is growing indication that Palestinian activists are turning away from alliances with bodies that count and towards building and renewing alliances with the struggles and movements of other indigenous and racialized peoples (see Bhandar and Ziadah 2016; Krebs and Olwan 2012; Morgensen 2012; Tatour 2016a; Waziyatawin 2012). Given the limited impact of decolonial solidarity activism on the Occupation, Palestinian activists are increasingly placing the onus on the Israeli activists to focus on decolonization within Israel (see Kaufman-Lacusta 2010; Alsaafin 2012). This demand is seen as a particularly daunting and difficult task by the Israeli activists given that, for most Israelis, the West Bank is a world apart despite being a forty-five-minute drive from Tel Aviv, and as such the concept of Israelis going to protests alongside Palestinians who are thought of as a terrorist threat, against a Wall that is supposed to keep Israelis safe from this threat, is perceived as 'immature' at best, and as 'irrational', 'crazy' and even 'dangerous' (Snitz 2013; see also Feinstein and Ben-Eliezer (2007) about how AATW activists are perceived by Israeli soldiers on duty around the Wall's route). Many AATW activists therefore described their relationship with mainstream Israeli society, including friends and relatives, as one of alienation and disconnection (see the writings of Assouline 2013; Edmonds 2013; Shapiro 2013; Wagner 2013).

In addition, Israeli society's rapid sociopolitical shift to the right over the past two decades has meant that confronting Israeli society with the possibility of decolonization is an increasingly difficult, if not impossible, task. Least of all because the Israeli state has moved to delegitimize and criminalize many of the activities which the anarchists and international solidarity activists have engaged with as a means to advocate for decolonization (Adalah 2011; Shapiro 2010; Landau 2018). The move to delegitimize this decolonial movement is the subject of the next chapter. This has led many Israeli decolonial activists to conclude that change from within Israeli society is a very distant possibility and that in the immediate future international pressure is the most effective strategy for sociopolitical change (see Assouline 2013; Ronnie Barkan in Dalla Negra 2012; Tali Shapiro in Kilroy 2011; Turner 2015; Weizman 2017).

Conclusion

Reflecting on nearly two decades of co-resistance against the Separation Wall in Palestine-Israel, this chapter identifies the strategic mobilization of vulnerability in non-violent protest actions against the Wall as the emergence and consolidation of a politics of decolonial solidarity. By participating in vulnerability-based solidarity, decolonial settler citizens who act in concert with the colonized-in-resistance can serve to unsettle the settler-colonial normative framing which legitimizes settler-colonial state violence against indigenous demands for decolonization. The shared experience of vulnerability-in-resistance serves to strengthen decolonial solidarity as a commitment to decolonization.

Nevertheless, the strategic mobilization and deployment of settler-citizenship and the racialized privilege of bodies that count in the service of decolonial solidarity can inadvertently reaffirm the very colonial racial hierarchies they seek to decolonize; rendering decolonial solidarity, and ultimately decolonization, in the context of Palestine-Israel somewhat paradoxical. Simultaneously, or rather as a consequence of participating in decolonial solidarity activism, decolonial activists' growing association and co-imbrication with the colonized-in-resistance render them as bodies out of place who become targets for colonial state violence. The above disassociation from the settler-colonial order warrants further exploration in terms of its sociopolitical implications for the future evolution of the struggle for decolonization in Palestine-Israel.

5

The backlash to the decolonial turn: 'Delegitimizing the delegitimizers'

The preceding chapters examined the evolution of critical political activism among Jewish-Israelis who have been historically active in protesting the 1967 Occupation into decolonial solidarity activism which is more closely aligned with Palestinian demands for decolonization, advocacy for the Palestinian right of return and insistence on equal citizenship. As the previous chapter concluded, the rapidly shrinking space for resistance within Palestine-Israel as a consequence of the Israeli state's backlash against any internal protest has meant that Jewish-Israeli activists have had to build stronger alliances with other decolonial solidarity activists in Europe, North America and elsewhere. The transnational movement for justice in Palestine-Israel is most clearly manifested in the praxis or the rhetoric and practices of the BDS movement. The widespread adoption of the BDS movement's aims and objectives in the past decade has been accompanied by a counter-trajectory in international politics characterized by the election of right-wing populist governments and the establishment of anti-decolonial civil society associations which appear to have a strong sway in national politics and policy.

This chapter advances a Gramscian analysis of the emergence of what is referred to as the 'backlash' to the decolonial turn. Much of this analysis is indebted to Antonio Gramsci's writing on civil society in his *Prison Notebooks* (1992). Although the majority of liberal and progressive scholarship on social movements emphasizes the progressive or counter-hegemonic nature of civil associations, for Gramsci civil society is an integral part of the state. Therefore, examining the role of hegemonic civil society formations is essential to understand how states are able to maintain dominant regimes of governance with the limited use of political violence against racially and/or politically privileged citizens; and by extension the extent to which they are successfully able to resist or delegitimize counter-hegemonic efforts at democratization and decolonization. This analysis also implies that successful decolonization may in fact require the emergence and evolution of a decolonial political society. There have been a number of instances in the past decade where the promise of such a decolonial political society was visible; albeit its emergence has been met with fierce opposition and resistance from the political and social centre-right. The promise of a decolonial political society was most notably evident in the social democratic turn in the British Labour Party under the leadership of Jeremy Corbyn and to a lesser extent Bernie Sanders's campaign for the Democratic Party presidential candidacy in the United States. The Joint List in Israel remains committed to the two-state solution. However, its growing political success may in fact signal the possibility for articulating an egalitarian agenda for cohabitation in Palestine-Israel. The political fate of and the extent to which life can remain liveable in the West Bank and Gaza Strip, the latter having been declared by the UN uninhabitable as of 2020, remain at stake.

As with all struggles for justice, success is not guaranteed and setbacks are inevitable; but students of social movements know that retreat does not imply defeat, and success comes in waves. The present rightward wave was preceded by the promise of a decolonial political society aligned with a progressive civil society making the possibility of decolonial cohabitation momentarily appear within close reach. As with all right-wing backlashes there will be progressive resistance characterized by a reinvigorated campaign for justice. In the present historical moment, the backlash against progressive civil society in Palestine-Israel and the transnational movement for BDS has been expressed as a set of legal, political and social campaigns which seek to delegitimize and criminalize BDS associated activism as an expression of 'anti-Semitism' and even 'terrorism'. In turn, BDS activists have had significant success in defending themselves against these charges on grounds of free speech and on the basis of their non-violent advocacy for justice and equality.

Civil society: An answer to war?

At the turn of the twenty-first century, Mary Kaldor declared global civil society an answer to war because 'the concept of civil society has always been linked to the notion of minimizing violence in social relations, to the public use of reason as a way of managing human affairs in place of submission based on fear and insecurity, or ideology and superstition' (2003: 3). She described civil society as 'global' in acknowledgement of its development, since 1989, into increasingly transnational forms related to the process of globalization – the process of globalization being perceived as contributing to the erosion of territorial state sovereignty. This global civil society is further defined by 'bottom up' or grassroots struggles for emancipatory goals, whether these are women's rights, environmental protection or peace, on the basis of 'governance based on consent where consent is generated through politics' (Kaldor 2003: 142).

Global civil society is further characterized by civil society groups putting pressure on economic and political institutions of authority through advocacy, campaigning and protest, in an effort to institute reform and/or the transformation of policy and practice at a global level (see also see Keck and Sikkink (1998]) on 'transnational advocacy networks'). These developments have in turn facilitated global public debates which offer 'the possibility of the voices of the victims of globalisation to be heard if not the votes' (Kaldor 2003: 148). On the other hand, Claire Mercer is quite critical of much of the literature on civil society, in particular the Anglophone literature on the role of NGOs in development, for subscribing to 'the normative ideal that civil society and NGOs are inherently "good things"; microcosms of the (liberal) democratic process, comprised of the grassroots, both separate and autonomous from the state, while acting as a "bulwark" against it' (2002: 9).

Mercer is also highly critical of liberal modernization theories and development discourses which tend to divide NGOs and civil society associations into 'good' and 'bad', or 'accommodating' versus 'resistant' to modernization, that is, neo-liberal agendas. Duffield (2007) further highlights the problematic role of humanitarian aid in global governance and its tacit complicity with state and corporate interests in the rise of asymetirc warfare in the Global South. This effectively challenges Kaldor's assertion that global civil society can be an answer to war and conflict:

> [Development] seeks to secure the non-insured through the disciplining and regulatory effects of self-reliance. Development aims to embed security within the world of peoples by making it sustainable (p. 124) ... unending

war is not primarily a military concern. It is more an indefinite and globalized counter insurgency campaign that utilises the civilian petty sovereignty of aid agencies to engage with questions of poverty and political instability. (Duffield 2007: 127)

Kaldor, however, excludes humanitarian NGOs from her definition of civil society because they are primarily concerned with service provision. Moreover, she highlights that since the 1980s social movements have undergone a processes of 'taming' 'whereby the authorities open up access to social movements and even take on some of their demands, and movements become institutionalized and professionalized' (2003: 145). Arundhati Roy (2004) refers to this process as 'the NGOisation of resistance' or the depoliticization and pacification of social movement activism.

However, as Joseph A. Buttigieg (2005) explains, much of the debate concerned with defining civil society as a force for the radical transformation of the status quo (counter-hegemonic), or as an easily co-opted or already functioning appendage of state and corporate interests (hegemonic), stems from a misunderstanding of Antonio Gramsci's concept of 'hegemony' and the subsequent conflation of civil society with oppositional and/or antigovernment movements. This misreading lends itself to an oversimplified view of the complex relationship between civil society and the state, or 'the people' and the government:

> Gramsci regarded civil society as an integral part of the state; in his view, civil society, far from being inimical to the state, is, in fact, its most resilient constitutive element, even though the most immediately visible aspect of the state is political society, with which it is all too often mistakenly identified. He was also convinced that the intricate, organic relationships between civil society and political society enable certain strata of society not only to gain dominance within the state but also, and more importantly, to maintain it, perpetuating the subalternity of other strata. To ignore or to set aside these crucial aspects of Gramsci's concept of civil society is tantamount to erasing the crucial differences that set his theory of the state apart from the classic liberal version. (Buttigieg 1995: 4)

As a consequence of the conflation between civil society and oppositional movements, contemporary academic debates concerned with the dichotomy between 'good' and 'bad' manifestations of civil society appear in many different guises, and often different authors' objections to others' definitions of civil society are at cross purposes. For some civil society is 'good' or 'counter-hegemonic' when it is manifested as a transnational social movement, while it is 'bad' or 'hegemonic' if it is NGOized (Roy 2004). For others, in the face of waning mass mobilization, particularly in the Global North prior to the re-emergence of public mass protest since 2010, NGOs which embody the values of 'progressive' social movements are considered 'good', even if in a 'tamed' version; while 'passive' NGOs, or NGOs which represent 'regressive' interests should arguably not be considered part of civil society (Kaldor 2003), or are alternatively defined as 'bad' forms of civil society (Walby 2009). Yet for others, all manifestations of autonomous non-state organizations are considered part of a modernizing and democratizing project which is arguably helping to build or strengthen civil society (for examples, see Mercer 2002).

In many respects, the 'progressive social movements' versus 'institutionalized civil society' distinction is redundant in the contemporary transnational context. For as Smith et al. (1997) emphasize, the successes of transnational activism depend on a combination of mobilizing structures, access to decision-making institutions and local, national and international structures of opportunity. Sidney Tarrow theorizes transnational social movements as a by-product of the process of internationalism, which he distinguishes from economic globalization, and defines as 'a dense triangular structure of relations among states, nonstate actors, and international institutions and the opportunities this produces for actors to engage in collective action at different levels of this system' (2005: 25).

The notion of internationalism highlights the fact that the majority of contemporary transnational activism is not necessarily concerned with supporting or opposing global capitalism, as embodied in the notion of globalization, but is rather rooted in domestic political concerns in relation to democratic and economic justice. Tarrow further defines transnational activists as 'people and groups who are rooted in specific national contexts, but who engage in contentious political activities that involve them in transnational networks of contact and conflict' (2005: 29). Examples of transnational movements based on internationalist concerns include not only diaspora and migrant movements but also peace, anti-war and human rights movements. The Palestinian-led BDS movement would be another example of Internationalism; whereby a dense network of transnational actors utilize political and financial dis/incentives in order to redefine the Israeli-Palestinian impasse and bring about its just resolution.

Therefore, social movements and civil society should not be envisaged as standing in opposition to or competition with each other. Rather, social movements function as umbrellas for ideas which can be articulated in different forms within civil society and/or autonomous activist associations, some of which may be in conflict with each other over objectives and strategies. For example, the transnational Palestinian Solidarity Movement (PSM), which has historically come under the slogans of 'Free Palestine' and/or 'End the Occupation' and more recently under the banner of 'Boycott, Divestment and Sanctions', has different and competing global, national and local manifestations. Some factions of this social movement call for a two-state solution, while others advocate for a single state; some believe their goal can be achieved through non-violent advocacy and campaigning, and others opt for more militant means; some groups organize in NGO forums, whilst others opt for grassroots mobilization and protest (see Abunimah 2014; Collins 2011). In essence, the PSM is transnational, heterogeneous and immeasurable as a whole. Its associated practices can be criminalized but it cannot be outlawed in its entirety.

Civil society on the other hand can only exist within legally identifiable and permissible national and/or transnational frameworks. In contrast to the relative autonomy and anonymity of transnational social movement actors, civil society can be held legally and politically accountable and is subject to regulation and supervision by the state, and other concerned institutions, that is, financial donors (see Kifukwe 2011). However, it is important to note that transnational movements which focus on the political transformation of a given state appear to be more successful at mobilizing long-term support and resources than those that focus on abstract values. The success of the South African anti-apartheid movement, which the BDS campaign draws inspiration from, can be contrasted with the failure of the anti-Iraq war movement which dissipated once the invasion had taken place because it failed to elaborate on concrete demands for political change (see Tarrow 2005).

The latter case also underscores the fact that the most successful transnational movements are those which are led and/or directed by the primary claims makers, or those affected by a given institution of power, with other transnational allies taking a position of solidarity. Therefore, transnational social movement activism remains rooted in domestic geopolitics while relying on transnational interconnection and structures of opportunity in order to bring about concrete local changes. Moreover, at the domestic level transnational social movement activism manifests as a civil society practice. Civil society is hereby understood as the key institutional site of contestation over sociopolitical frames and discourses characterized by private organizations of citizens that are separate from, yet imbricated with, the state and economy (see Walby 2009). The domain of civil society, therefore, includes religious institutions, political parties, trade unions and other professional associations, as well as humanitarian and advocacy NGOs, any of which can be defined as active, passive, progressive or regressive depending on one's perspective. Given that the state remains the key institutional site for the guarantee and security of human rights and their violation, transnational civil society continues to play an instrumental role in challenging the state's right to wage violence with complete impunity against people in the territories it has jurisdiction over (see Kaldor 2003; Nash 2009).

Studying critical Israeli activism from the perspective of decolonial critical theories can, therefore, better account for the often neglected, emergent and obscured 'postcolonial civil society' which is characterized by an ongoing 'conversation about the impact of hegemony, colonial praxis, the global economy and the reconstruction of rights, needs and identities' (Richmond 2011: 432). Nevertheless, these civil society networks need to be approached with caution for while characterized by a multiplicity of transnational actors, they are not even, and are even less equal. For Gramsci 'civil society in the modern liberal State is the arena wherein the prevailing hegemony is constantly being reinforced, not just contested' (Buttigieg 2005: 38). Given the transnational history of imperialism and ongoing settler colonialism, transnational civil society is deeply implicated in and structured by hierarchies of power and privilege which dictate unequal capacity to access the resources which would enable effective action in relation to authoritative regimes.

This is certainly the case in Palestine-Israel where the geopolitical dominance of settler-colonial dispossession continues to deny and repress Palestinian political agency and demands for decolonization. It is therefore not unreasonable to wonder why focus on and pay attention to critical and decolonial Jewish-Israeli activism given its small and marginal status within Israeli society. After all there has been very little evidence for any meaningful mainstream Israeli civil society engagement with Palestinian calls for justice since the failure of the Oslo Accords and the outbreak of the Al Aqsa Intifada. Since 2000 and the spread of right-wing politics, the left in Israel is barely in existence. The concept of the Israeli left has itself changed dramatically over time. During the pre-state settlement project and later in the early state years, the left was of a nationalistic persuasion, primarily interested in consolidating Jewish workers' interests in spite of and against Palestinian Arab workers in Palestine (see Pappé 2004; Shafir 2005). In the 1990s the Israeli left reinvented itself by incorporating more culturalist concerns, in line with other leftist movements in Europe and North America at the time. During that period the New Left became associated with the desire to return to the pre-1967 borders and the notion of a two-state solution. Over two decades later what remains of the Israeli liberal left can hardly be called either a cultural or economic left. Israeli society is deeply stratified both along ethno-classist lines, and even more so with respect to the Palestinians who are seen as radically other. In a 2001 report written in the midst of the Second Intifada, and the imminent election of Ariel Sharon to the post of Israel's Prime Minister, Lindsey Hilsum wrote:

> In December [2000], after Yasser Arafat raised again the question of Palestinian refugees forced into exile when Israel was founded in 1948, a group of left-wing writers and artists, including novelists Amos Oz and Meir Shalev, signed a petition declaring their opposition to the right of return. (Hilsum 2001: 23)

The report goes on to explain how many members of the Peace Now movement, the largest and oldest peace movement in Israel, are increasingly adopting ultra-right-wing rhetoric of a population transfer of the Arab citizens of Israel, rightly leading the report to conclude that this turn to the right signalled 'the death of the Israeli left'. It is arguably no longer possible to speak of a large left-wing peace movement in Israel. The left-associated peace movement was never anti-racist as such; after all, the notion of two ethno-states for two peoples relies on a racialized logic. However, the mainstream liberal left seems to have become silent and taken a backseat even on the subject of a two-state solution, with the right-wing demand for a Greater Israel in Palestine-Israel becoming an increasing reality on the ground in the Occupied Territories, accompanied by continuous rhetoric about transferring Palestinian citizens out of Israel.

Lintl (2016) further attributes the shift to the right to widespread disappointment and disenchantment with the peace process that has also led to the growth and mainstreaming of radical-right populism reflected in the election of right-wing coalition governments since 2009. More recently, the emergence and consolidation of a radical-right populist consensus in Israeli electoral politics has also had the unintended consequence of making the Joint List of Palestinian MKs the third largest political block in Israel's Parliament and in effect the largest opposition party. The Joint List was formed as a response to a law passed ahead of the 2015 election which raised the electoral threshold for parliamentary seats in effect threatening the electoral viability of minority parties. Kook (2017) argues that the significance and success of the Joint List can be attributed to their advocacy for policies which champion social justice and social, political and economic well-being for all citizens. This has attracted a significant number of Jewish-Israeli voters who have turned away from the traditional Zionist liberal left. The shifting political terrain in Israeli party politics away from the centrality of the Zionist liberal left as the only alternative to the Zionist right points to the possibility of the mainstreaming of a multicultural democratic one-state as a viable and legitimate option (see also Boehm 2020). Although it should be noted that at present the Joint List remains formally committed to a two-state solution.

Alongside this sociopolitical development, by breaking away from the Zionist hegemony and aligning themselves with the BDS movement and its demands for decolonization, critical and decolonial Jewish-Israeli activists have, according to Elian Weizman (2017), advanced a Gramscian 'steady war of position', in other words they are advancing a range of critical and radical ideas for change, in the hope to decolonize the Jewish-Israeli imagination so as to bring about structural and systemic change. Despite this, the transnational popularization of the BDS movement has had contradictory and unintended effects on Israeli society. The first of these consequences has been the growth of a siege mentality among Israeli politicians and the public expressed in the election and entrenchment of ultra-right-wing parties in Israel's coalition governments since 2009 (Lintl 2016), and the proliferation of draconian laws designed to curb critical speech and assembly and punish anti-occupation and decolonial activism (see Asseburg 2017; Jamal 2018; Waxman 2016).

The second of these unfortunate consequences is the growth of ultra-nationalist right-wing social movements who target critical Israeli civil society, human rights advocates and transnational BDS activists with counter-delegitimation campaigns. They instigate boycotts against critical individuals, and increasingly seek to reframe criticisms of Israel as a 'Jewish state', and support for one-person/one-vote democratic state as 'anti-Semitic', and/or 'supporting terrorism' (see Amnesty International 2016; Dayan 2019; Gordon 2014; Nashif and Naamneh 2016; Lamarche 2019). This development has been termed 'the rise of bad civil society' (Jamal 2018) and stems from the emergence of NGOs such as NGO Monitor (est. 2001) and Im Tirtzu (est. 2006) in Israel, with corresponding Jewish-diaspora-led organizations such as StandWithUs (est. 2001 in the United States) which boasts eighteen international chapters including in the UK and Canada (see StandWithUs website) and Campus Watch USA (est. 2002). These organizations overwhelmingly operate on university campuses and target staff and students who are critical of Israeli policies, advocate for Palestinian human rights and/or are active in BDS advocacy.

These NGOs' campaigns of accusations and allegations, complaints and demands to have faculty fired for their political beliefs and critical expression have had various degrees of success in the United States and Israel, and to a lesser degree in Europe (see various cases in Center for Constitutional Rights' report: *The Palestine Exception to Free Speech* 2015). Many of the tactics employed by these right-wing civil society organizations appear to actively mirror BDS activism in terms of using the tactics of boycott and public protest; although it should be noted that BDS does not target individuals for boycott. The proponents of counter-BDS campaigns claim to seek to expose and combat racially motivated criticisms against Israel as anti-Semitic through the strategy of 'delegitimising the delegitimisers' (see Peled 2013). These campaigns have had considerable national and international success in the past decade.

Delegitimizing democracy: Lawfare and the rise of 'bad civil society'

Despite their claim to act as independent social movement activists and organizations (for an example of the discourses of the proponents of this strategy see Plaut 2011) many of the aforementioned groups have close links to the Israeli government and have been responsible for instigating and supporting several pieces of legislation designed to target left-wing and critical Israeli activists and organizations (see Dayan 2019; Jamal 2018; Lamarche 2019). Since 2011 the Israeli government has debated numerous bills and passed several legislations designed to curtail critical activism and punish those engaging in it. These include the 2011 'Boycott Law' which criminalizes Israelis who call for the boycott of Israel or the Israeli settlements in the Occupied Territories.

The 2011 Anti-Boycott Law makes any Israeli individual or organization who/which support or advocate boycott of Israel or the settlements in the Occupied Territories subject to private legal prosecution. Israeli proponents of BDS face financial penalties not only if an organization suffers financial loss because of a boycott action, but even if it feels it might suffer financial loss. At the time, leading international human rights organizations criticized the law for infringing on freedom of expression (Amnesty International 2011; Human Rights Watch 2011). Internal critics also argued that the law effectively legitimizes and annexes the settlements to Israel (Lis 2011). The law was also originally criticized by senior members of the right-leaning think tank, the Reut Institute, who issued a statement arguing that the Anti-Boycott Law gives more legitimacy to the international movement for boycott and further helps to delegitimize Israel as a democratic state: 'The Boycott Law ... does not properly address the de-legitimization phenomenon, as the law is territorial in its application and yet the de-legitimization campaign is global, primarily operating beyond Israel's borders' (Keidar and Shayshon 2011: n.p.). The case of the Israeli Anti-Boycott Law illustrates succinctly the Gramscian conceptualization of civil society as the terrain in which dominant discourses are continuously contested and reinforced.

Moreover, civil society does not function as a field separate from and in opposition to the state, but rather its activities are constrained, controlled and even subject to permission and punishment by the government of the state within which it functions. Civil society actors are therefore entangled in complex webs of geopolitics and are subject to the very governance regimes they seek to challenge and hold to account. The 2016 'NGO Law' is another case which further challenges some of the liberal assumptions contained within a lot of literature on civil society that progressive civil society is able to democratize the state by engaging in transnational advocacy networks which promote compliance with international human rights norms (for example see Keck and Sikkink (1998)). The NGO law requires Israeli NGOs to declare all funding from foreign governments or 'foreign governmental entities', including a proposed clause which was struck down and would have required NGO representatives to wear badges declaring their foreign government donors when speaking in the Knesset (see Asseburg 2017; Jamal 2018; Amnesty International 2016). This law overwhelmingly targets left-wing, human rights and critical NGOs as right-wing counterparts tend to receive funding from private individual donors. Critics of the law have argued that the law was designed precisely to single-out, demonize and delegitimize critical human rights and civil society organizations as a 'fifth column', 'foreign agents' and a 'security threat' to the Israeli state (see Gordon 2014; Nashif and Naamneh 2016; Middle East Monitor 2018; Waxman 2016).

Neve Gordon (2014) identifies this trend as 'lawfare' whereby right-wing politicians and NGOs are increasingly framing human rights work as a 'security threat'. The (un)intended consequence of this is the active delegitimation of human rights and international law. In essence, the state is reasserting its Weberian right to sovereign violence and the Schmittian right to declare its enemies and the state of exception with almost total impunity (see Agamben 2005; Owen and Strong 2004). This backlash against critical civil society was spearheaded by right-wing NGOs, politicians and media outlets in the wake of the UN Fact-Finding Mission on the Gaza Conflict (2009), or the Goldstone Commission, which Khoury-Bisharat (2019) describes as 'the unintended consequences' of engaging with international legal instruments. Some of these unintended consequences have included civil society campaigners being smeared in the media, receiving physical threats and increasingly withdrawing from international co-operation with the UN and EU in order to avoid charges of disloyalty and treason so as to be able to continue operating at the domestic level. Another example of the state's resistance to oversight from human rights organizations and the international legal community is the expulsion in 2019 of the director of Human Rights Watch, Omar Shakir, under another anti-BDS law from 2017 which bars entry to people who advocate for a boycott of Israel or the settlements in the Occupied Territories (Human Rights Watch 2019).

The delegitimation campaign against critical Israeli and international human rights NGOs based in Palestine-Israel has gone international and is increasingly targeting donor EU member-states to demand that they defund and/or stop working with human rights advocates in Palestine-Israel. Israel's 2018 Nation State Law and the widely criticized US administration's 2020 'Deal of the Century' proposal for a de facto 'apartheid-like' one-state solution (see criticisms of the plan by Jewish Voice for Peace as reported in the Middle East Eye 2020) signal the growing national and international normalization and acceptance of these right-wing ultra-nationalist discourses. These developments also testify to the growing delegitimation of international law and human rights (see Gordon 2014), and the public legitimation of Israel's settler-colonial expansion and Palestinian dispossession (see Amnesty International UK 2020a).

That the legitimation of Israel's settler colonialism and the delegitimation of human rights and democracy is taking place with the public support of the US government, itself a long-standing and established settler colony, is not insignificant, and does not bode well for the trajectory of contemporary international governance and the impact it is having and will have on citizenship, human rights and human security. More specifically, within Palestine-Israel, the immediate consequences of a right-wing hegemony in public and political life is the increasing insecurity felt by Palestinian citizens and Palestinian rights NGOs and organizations in the face of threats to their citizenship, well-being and their right to political expression and participation (see Nashif and Naamneh 2016). The right-wing demand for 'loyalty' to the Jewish state is clearly designed to target non-Jewish citizens who are already heavily disenfranchised and discriminated against due to being excluded from belonging in the dominant ethnonation. However, (dis)loyalty may also become the litmus test for citizenship rights for Jewish-Israelis who advocate for democracy over ethnocracy and against apartheid (see Waxman 2016). Alongside targeting progressive civil society, right-wing NGOs have also been active in waging 'a war of position' vis-à-vis progressive and critical academics in Israel and abroad. From a Gramscian perspective this can be straightforwardly analysed as a contestation over the production and legitimation of the Zionist hegemony.

The Israeli NGO Im Tirtzu (2011) for example produced a lengthy report on the political science department of Ben Gurion University going so far as to name faculty members for their support of the boycott, counting who is being cited in module reading lists on the basis of whether they are Zionist or post-Zionist, whether they are critical of Israel or not (see 'Politicization at Ben Gurion University' 2011). Such reports are designed to police critical scholars on the basis of 'bias' and have been accompanied by so-far unsuccessful campaigns, similar to the NGO laws, who alongside right-wing politicians seek to make it a fireable offence to express any political opinion in the classroom (see Jamal 2018). Aside from being clearly designed to deny political expression to critical academics, such proposals are based on a bizarre and contradictory premise that uncritical support for the politics and policies of a government or state is somehow 'apolitical' and 'unbiased' and that only agreement with the status quo and the reproduction of dominant discourses and ideologies count as 'legitimate' scholarship and 'proper' knowledge. This perspective also appears to be surprisingly anti-intellectual and ahistorical in as far as it fails to acknowledge that critique of the status quo and a desire to democratize dominant institutions are fundamental characteristics of a democratic and/or democratizing society. Consequently, by rendering critique as a security and/or existential threat to the status quo, democracy and democratic expression are delegitimized in the process. This anti-democratic logic has transnational counterparts in growing 'anti-expertise' sentiments in North America and Europe where domestic right-wing and pro-Israel groups are also increasingly targeting scholars critical of Israel using a range of existing and proposed security and counter-terrorism legislation (for examples see Abunimah 2014).

Transnationalizing the delegitimation campaign

In February 2015, the Counter Terrorism and Security Act 2015 put the Prevent Duty on a statutory basis for the first time, imposing an obligation on public bodies in the UK (including universities, colleges, nurseries, prisons and the NHS) to have 'due regard to the need to prevent people from being drawn into terrorism'. The Prevent strategy has long been subjected to criticisms for its problematic inclusion of support for the Palestinian cause as a sign of potential 'radicalization' which may lead to 'violent extremism'. The law, which also unironically considers being critical of Prevent to be a sign of potential radicalization, has from its inception been widely criticized by academics, trade unions, student unions and civil society organizations for its potential to criminalize and pathologize legitimate expressions of political opinion such as support for human rights, including Palestinian human rights, freedom of speech, including the freedom to express criticisms of Israel's policies against the Palestinians, as well as the right to express criticisms against the UK government for passing problematic legislation which may have the (un)intended consequences of threatening to and potentially criminalizing critical speech on a range of issues including foreign policy, racial discrimination, human rights and/or democracy more generally (see McVeigh 2015; Nagdee 2019; Ross 2016).

In the era of a permanent war-against-terror, legislation such as Prevent is neither unique nor exceptional. The relevance of its discussion pertains to the fact that since its inauguration in 2015 this legislation has been used to curtail speech and assembly related to Palestine on UK campuses exemplified by demands by pro-Israel groups to have events on campus cancelled, the increasing securitization of student-run events, public accusations and complaints being made against academics who speak, research or teach on Palestine (see Bouattia 2018 and 2019; Kite, Salvoni and Kinder 2019). While the consequences of being 'reported' under Prevent often result in little more than lengthy investigations which are often psychologically distressing for the accused but rarely result in serious consequences (see Middle East Monitor 2020), the ongoing campaign to have statutory bodies adopt the International Holocaust Remembrance Alliance (IHRA) definition of anti-Semitism has had a far more chilling effect on free speech.

Since 2017 the UK government has adopted the IHRA definition of anti-Semitism and it is widely accepted that the definition requires legal interpretation. In a legal opinion by Hugh Tomlinson QC (Free Speech on Israel 2017), he criticized the definition for being 'unclear' and 'confusing' and makes the case that adoption of the IHRA definition may in fact contravene article 10(2) of the European Convention on Human Rights which guarantees free speech (even if that speech is found to be offensive). The definition, which begins with the words 'Anti-Semitism is a certain perception of Jews, which may be expressed as hatred towards Jews', is followed by a list of eleven examples which include:

- Denying the Jewish people their right to self-determination, e.g., by claiming that the existence of a State of Israel is a racist endeavor.
- Applying double standards by requiring of it [Israel] a behavior not expected or demanded of any other democratic nation. (see IHRA website)

The above examples can be interpreted as problematic least of all because in the first instance they conflate a people's right to self-determine with state sovereignty and a state project. This is problematic in that it can be used to set a precedent for political systems which privilege the national rights of dominant ethno-religious groups over cultural and minority ethnic citizens' rights in other states; including states which self-define as democratic. The inadvertent consequence of this is that 'Jewish self-determination' cannot be perceived as collective self-representation and/or cultural self-government taking place in a multicultural state and society, whether this is in Israel, Palestine-Israel or elsewhere. Tying any state project to a single nationality or ethno-religious group also rejects the possibility that a state may in fact embrace equal citizenship in a multicultural or a multi-ethnic state. Moreover, advocacy for equal citizenship in a multicultural and multi-ethnic State of Israel should not be interpreted as a rejection of 'Jewish self-determination'. This is why the chapter which addresses the question of the one state places emphasis on self-determination as cultural, social and political citizenship. Moreover, the demand for equal citizenship is a demand that has been placed on all democratic states throughout the history of democracy and is an essential part of the process of democratization. In addition, the BDS movement has emphasized that its stated goal is equality and its supporters remain divided on a particular state position.

Alongside this development, BDS activism across Europe and North America has faced a similar campaign of delegitimation, increasing criminalization and a concerted effort to reframe its intentions as driven by anti-Semitism or even as an expression of anti-Semitism. As Michiel Bot (2019) outlines, since 2014 over a hundred pieces of anti-BDS legislation have been enacted at the local, state and federal level in the United States, including the 2019 'Combating BDS Act' passed by the Senate which essentially amounts to 'a boycott of the boycotters' and which bars individual citizens from public employment and welfare assistance on the basis of their advocacy of BDS. When challenged in court some of these laws have been found to violate constitutional rights to free speech and assembly. In the UK, in 2016 a ministerial statutory guidance was issued prohibiting local authorities from engaging in boycott and sanctions unless such a directive has been directly issued by the government. Since 2016 there have been several criminal prosecutions against BDS activists in France and Germany, and in 2019 the German parliament passed a resolution defining BDS campaigns as anti-Semitic. Several of the convictions under these legislations have since been overturned. In 2020 the European Court of Human Rights declared the convictions of several French activists to be in contravention of their right to free speech (Amnesty International UK 2020b). The European Legal Support Centre established in 2019 has also had several victories in court successfully challenging motions that condemn BDS campaigns as anti-Semitic as violating constitutional rights to freedom of expression and assembly (see website).

Bot (2019) makes a robust case for the deeply problematic nature of these developments as they amount to the instrumentalization of the law to frame BDS as discriminatory. Such arguments amount to a gross misrepresentation of a movement which in essence champions civic equality and multicultural democracy and which is supported by critical Jewish-Israelis as well as Jewish-heritage and Jewish-identified citizens in the United States, the UK, Germany, France, the rest of Europe and North America. Moreover, the movement draws on a long and well-established history of the use of the boycott tactics by anti-colonial, anti-apartheid and civil rights movements in India, South Africa and the US South during segregation (Bot 2019; Dean 2019; Singh 2019). The Black Lives Matter and BDS movements can be seen as contemporary expressions of the strategic use of the tactic of boycott by progressive social movements. Moreover, in their personal capacity individuals should have the right to voice an opinion about matters of belief, including political belief. This does not necessarily mean that others may agree with their perspective or that they should adopt their advocacy and opinions. The aims and objectives of a movement are only as significant as the number of people who choose to adopt the particular stance. One can hope to persuade but agreement is not guaranteed. However, what is presently and needs to remain guaranteed is the right to free speech.

In essence, framing BDS as discriminatory serves to delegitimize legitimate protest against racial discrimination and dispossession in Palestine-Israel. It also closes down civic avenues for engaged citizens to participate in politics as active agents of local, national and transnational change, and, in the process, it also delegitimizes progressive civil society and multicultural democracy in Europe and North America. What we are witnessing in the contemporary moment is powerful former colonial and current settler-colonial states, which have histories of colonialism and, in many instances, continue to engage in ongoing practices of racialized discrimination against segments of their domestic populations, coming together in solidarity with each other to form an alliance in order to reassert a Schmittian notion of sovereignty, and who seek to diminish the sphere of civil society so as to resist democratization and decolonization. In that sense the backlash against BDS, Palestinian human rights and progressive transnational civil society needs to be understood as part of a broader rightward trajectory in international politics (see Schechter 2017).

From a Gramscian perspective progressive civil society is currently losing a battle in the war of position vis-à-vis the legitimacy of colonialism, exclusivist ethnonationalism and the desirability of democracy. Palestinian activists have, therefore, for the past decade focused on renewing and building alliances with other racialized populations and decolonial movements in North America in order to highlight the transnational interconnectedness of colonized people in the settler-colonial present (Anti-Blackness Roundtable 2015; Estes 2019). Nevertheless, movements such as Black Lives Matter and indigenous resistance to settler colonial dispossession have also faced a crackdown through misrepresentation and criminalization since 2016 (see Estes 2019; Taylor 2016). Activism against environmental destruction has also been the target of attempts at criminalization, and public space as a sphere for political assembly has been more or less successfully securitized in the UK (see BBC News 2019; Gayle 2019).

What is becoming increasingly clear is the need for the emergence of a concerted transnational social movement alliance to work towards developing strategies to resist the backlash against progressive civil society not only in relation to BDS activism and Palestinian human rights but in order to defend the right to political mobilization more broadly. Perhaps we can learn from and reappropriate the tactics of right-wing NGOs, by building relationships and alliances with critical politicians and members of the judiciary, campaigning to change draconian laws, as well as developing a legal strategy to resist lawfare attacks on free speech and association in the short to medium term. It is also increasingly clear that we need to become more aggressive about countering smears and reputational attacks against activists, academics and progressive public figures. Such alliances will require the acquisition and mobilization of existing and new expertise. This strategy will be costly in terms of time, energy and resources, but what is at stake is too dear to abandon in the face of right-wing attack. What is at stake is the security of social democracy, human rights and justice.

Conclusion

This chapter examined the backlash against progressive civil society as a consequence of the rise of right-wing pro-Israel NGOs and social movements in Israel, Europe and North America. The rise of right-wing social movements is a direct consequence of a general rightward direction in international politics. The rightward direction of international politics is characterized by ethnocentrism, national chauvinism, militarism and increasing attacks on the legitimacy of liberal notions of free speech and association, participatory democracy through protest action, and equal rights for minoritized citizens. Simultaneously, there has been a systematic campaign to delegitimize as 'anti-Semitic' the advocacy efforts of the BDS movement to democratize, decolonize and bring about equality in Palestine-Israel. This delegitimation effort has been met with support by numerous governments, but it is also increasingly facing resistance by progressive civil society which insists on the right to utilize free speech in order to advocate for justice, fairness and equality. A positive outcome of this rightward trajectory is that it is increasing and strengthening transnational links between Palestinians, decolonial Jewish-Israelis and those who stand in solidarity with their struggle for justice.

Conclusion

At the time of writing Israel has temporarily halted its formal annexation of large parts of the occupied West Bank amidst an international diplomatic and civil society outcry (see AlJazeera 2020; BBC News 2020; UNCHR 2020). A range of op-ed pieces decrying the end of the two-state solution have been authored by critics ranging from the moderate right to the liberal left and beyond (for example see Beinart 2020; Boehm 2020; Yoffie 2020). Sounding the death knell for the two-state solution is now a 20-year-old endeavour. In reality, as this monograph calls to attention, the two-state solution has never been on the cards beyond diplomatic rhetoric designed to keep Israel's political advantage over the Palestinians. The proposed annexation is in contravention of international law as has been Israel's 53-year-old Occupation of the Gaza Strip and West Bank. This move has revealed 'the peace process' as a mirage. It has also dealt a substantive blow to the legitimacy of any sort of international liberal-Zionist advocacy for *a Jewish and democratic state* coexisting alongside a territorially compromised Palestinian state in some of the West Bank and Gaza Strip (see Yoffie 2020). In turn this has also revealed the ideological chasm between liberal-Zionist supporters of the State of Israel abroad and the ever more radical-right-populism characterizing Israel's internal social and political landscape. That this blow to the liberal-Zionist international consensus has been dealt at the back of a decade-long campaign to delegitimize any progressive civil society criticism of Israel's Occupation, colonization and human rights violations is not insignificant and should call for some serious soul searching among anyone but the most radical-right advocate for Israel.

This monograph offers a modest opportunity for a critical reflection on the reality on the ground and the opportunities to re-evaluate the way forward offered by the efforts of a small number of critical Jewish-Israelis who have been struggling to decolonize their thinking and practice in order to move beyond the current impasse. The situation which Palestine-Israel has reached is no longer a question of a two- versus one-state solution. It is a question of, on the one hand, succumbing to a Jewish-dominated state determined to colonize, occupy and annex as much territory for its own benefit at the expense of Palestinian human rights and sovereignty. On the other hand, lies the only just alternative option: a transnational campaign for a democratic one-state, or alternatively there needs to be a reinvigorated campaign for two democratic states in which Jewish-Israelis, Palestinians and all other minority ethnic residents live as equals. Neither state option excludes the demand for and right to equal citizenship. Of the three case study groups examined in this book only Zochrot and ICAHD have considered the democratic one-state option. To begin with the decolonial activism of the Anarchists Against the Wall is a fundamental stance that any advocate for decolonization and equal citizenship in Palestine-Israel has to undertake to work towards, irrespective of the state solution. In fact, without undertaking the necessary work to decolonize one's thinking and practice the violence of the settler-colonial present will remain and intensify.

Unlearning official state-sponsored narratives and acknowledging the narratives of the dispossessed Palestinians has been an integral aspect of undertaking decolonial praxis for all of the activist groups discussed in this book. Zochrot has made Nakba commemoration and education a cornerstone of their work for this very reason. ICAHD's long-standing campaign of grassroots resistance to house demolitions has been an opportunity to reflect on the nature of the Occupation as a settler-colonial project. None of these activists have come straightforwardly to a decolonial perspective and/or advocacy for a democratic one-state. The unlearning process has been slow and painstaking, at times full of tensions and contradictions. Yet, the backlash such activism has faced within Palestine-Israel and abroad suggests that it is perceived as a serious threat by those who advocate for and/or uncritically defend Israel's settler colonialism and Palestinian dispossession.

The backlash against the movement for justice in Palestine-Israel is a consequence of the breakdown in the international liberal-Zionist consensus within and outside the State of Israel. As Boehm (2020) highlights this backlash is also spurred on by the fact that left-leaning Jewish-Israelis in general, and not only activists, are increasingly turning to vote for the Palestinian block within the 1948 territories and what attracts them is precisely policies which champion equality, diversity and cohabitation. This signals unprecedented convergence between Jewish-Israelis and the Palestinian citizens of Israel which could potentially open up precisely the sort of mainstream space which is needed for a critical and collective discussion on decolonization and the one state. This is currently not possible within the political mainstream given that the Nation State Law has criminalized such a conversation. However, the Nation State Law is being challenged, and if left-wing Jewish and Palestinian Israelis organize collectively to campaign to have it revoked this would further strengthen their alliance and would expand the possibility to have an open conversation about a range of other issues including the right of return and equal citizenship.

At present these sorts of conversations are taking place internationally through the BDS movement which is also facing a backlash precisely because it is a platform for such a decolonial alliance. The backlash is also taking place in the context of a rightward trajectory in international politics and civil society which has gathered pace since around 2015. This global swing to the right can partially be attributed to the aftermath of the 2008 global financial crash which ushered in a decade of austerity-type policies across the Global North and South.

At the time of concluding this manuscript the world is facing one of its biggest challenges of the century. The coronavirus pandemic is intensifying global, regional and national inequalities in terms of mortality, health and employment. Minority ethnic citizens, migrants and colonized populations are bearing the brunt of poor health outcomes and lack of or limited access to adequate healthcare and welfare assistance. This is reflected in global mortality statistics which are characterized by a classed and racialized valuation of life and wellbeing. The lockdowns and social distancing measures which have been put in place by governments to deal with the severity of a deadly and disabling virus have intensified surveillance practices. Social distancing measures have not, however, dampened social mobilization. The Black Lives Matter Movement in particular has seen a resurgence and reinvigoration characterized by mass street protests and solidarity rallies across North America and Europe.

Israel within its 1948 borders has also seen largescale mobilization in protest against political corruption and economic instability. Public focus on what is set to be the biggest global economic recession on record closely mirrors the demands of the 2011 social justice protests. The present movement is diverse in terms of its Jewish-Israeli sociopolitical constituency; yet despite the political significance of the paused annexation plan, the Occupation is not explicitly named as a priority for the movement. This may of course change if the Israeli government decides to resume its annexation. In the present moment it is difficult to foresee if the decolonial agenda can or will play a significant part in the evolution of this movement or whether it requires the mobilization of a different sociopolitical constituency. As with all pivotal moments which are likely to reinvigorate a social movement this may require a 'contentious moment' (see Tarrow 2011) or a one-off event of a tragic and/or contested nature which becomes a symbol for transnational political action. The murder of George Floyd in the summer of 2020 has been such a moment for the transnational reinvigoration of the Black Lives Matter Movement. Such moments are often unpredictable, unforeseen and undesirable, as in an ideal situation justice will be served without contention. However, contentious moments offer some hope as they highlight that all moments of crisis and uncertainty represent opportunities for justice and progressive social change.

Notes

Introduction

This introduction chapter is based on Teodora Todorova, 'Vulnerability as a politics of decolonial solidarity: The case of the Anarchists Against the Wall', *Identities*, 27 (3) (2019): 321–38, DOI: 10.1080/1070289X.2019.1647663, reprinted with permission by Taylor and Francis; Teodora Todorova, 'Reframing bi-nationalism in Palestine-Israel as a process of settler decolonisation', *Antipode*, 47 (5) (2015): 1367–87, DOI: 10.1111/anti.12153, reproduced with permission by John Wiley and Sons.

1. Similarly to Smith, I use the concept 'myth' not to connote a 'false' or 'fabricated' account of history but rather 'a widely held view of the past which has helped to shape and explain the present' (Smith 2000: 2).
2. An 'ethnocracy' is a state which is neither democratic nor authoritarian 'yet facilitates non-democratic seizure of the country and polity by one ethnic group … Ethnocracies despite exhibiting several democratic features, lack a democratic structure. As such they tend to breach key democratic tenets, such as equal citizenship, the existence of a territorial political community (demos), universal suffrage, and protection against the tyranny of the majority' (Yiftachel 2010: 270).
3. The call for BDS is supported by a number of critical Israeli groups and individuals including the signatories of Boycott From Within (BFW), Anarchists Against the Wall (AATW), the Israeli Committee Against House Demolitions (ICAHD), Zochrot and the Coalition of Women for Peace, an umbrella organization of anti-militarist, feminist women's groups.
4. The Nakba refers to the catastrophic events of 1947–9 during which the majority of the Palestinian population was displaced in the wake of the establishment of the State of Israel.
5. The Palestinian refugees' right of return is based on the UN resolution 194, 'The United Nations General Assembly adopts resolution 194 (III), resolving that 'refugees wishing to return to their homes and live at peace with their neighbours should be permitted to do so at the earliest practicable date, and that compensation should be paid for the property of those choosing not to return and for loss of or damage to property which, under principles of international law or equity, should be made good by the Governments or authorities responsible' (see https://www.unrwa.org/content/resolution-194).

6 Article 49 of the Fourth Geneva Convention stipulates, 'Individual or mass forcible transfers, as well as deportations of protected persons from occupied territory to the territory of the Occupying Power or to that of any other country, occupied or not, are prohibited, regardless of their motive ... The Occupying Power shall not deport or transfer parts of its own civilian population into the territory it occupies.' See https://www.icrc.org/ihl/ WebART/380-600056.

7 This refers to the settler-colonial tendency to eliminate or exterminate the indigenous population in the process of establishing its claim to the land in order to govern unchallenged (see Veracini 2010; Wolfe 2006).

8 This standpoint is greatly indebted to the work of Hannah Arendt ([1951] 2017, 1958, 1970, 2007) and David Harvey (2009).

1 Theorizing the Israeli settler colony

1 Jewish presence in Palestine predates Zionist immigration post-1882. In 1850 the Jewish population of Ottoman Palestine was estimated at 4 per cent (Schölch 1985: 503). British Mandate surveys place the Jewish population of Palestine at 11 per cent in 1922 and 31 per cent in 1945, the population increase reflecting immigration trends (Institute for Palestine Studies 1991).

2 B'Tselem (2017), 'Planning Policy in the West Bank'. https://www.btselem.org/planning_and_building.

3 Personal notes from the Russell Tribunal on Palestine, International session on corporate complicity in Israel's Occupation (20 November 2010).

4 See http://december18th.org/category/Testimonials/.

2 Bearing witness to Al Nakba in a time of denial: The case of Zochrot (Remembering)

This chapter is based on Teodora Todorova, 'Bearing witness to Al Nakba in a time of denial', in *Narrating Conflict in the Middle East: Discourse, Image and Communication Practices in Lebanon and Palestine*, edited by Dina Matar and Zahera Harb (London: I.B. Tauris, 2013), pp. 248–70, used by permission of Bloomsbury Publishing.

1 UN GAR 181 – 'United Nations General Assembly Resoloution 181 (II). 29 November 1947)'. https://unispal.un.org/DPA/DPR/unispal.nsf/0/7F0AF2BD897689B785256C330061D253.

2 On the importance of myths or dominant narratives for national storytelling see Smith (2000).
3 '**Land & Housing Rights:** The Absentee Property Law declares that anyone who left the country in 1948 is an absentee, and that his/her property comes under the control of the State. This Law was used only against Arabs [Palestinians], and even in reference to people who remained in the country but who were compelled to leave their land. These individuals are called "present absentees". The Defence (Emergency) Regulation 125 authorizes the military commander to declare land to be a "closed area." Once he so declares, no person is allowed to enter or to leave the area. By this regulation, the population of tens of Arab villages became uprooted. There is no uprooted Jewish population in the State. The National Planning & Building Law prohibits the provision of basic services such as water and electricity to tens of unrecognized Arab villages in the State. Although these villages existed before the State's establishment, the main purpose of the law is to force the people to leave their villages and move to government-planned areas. There are no unrecognized Jewish villages in Israel' (Adalah, Legal Centre for Arab Minority Rights in Israel, Report to UN CERD 1998: 2, http://www.adalah.org/eng/intladvocacy/cerd-major-finding-march98.pdf).
4 Al Nakba is annually commemorated on 14 May according to the Gregorian calendar, while Israel's Independence Day celebrations are annually held on 5 Iyar according to the Hebrew calendar. The two dates do not always coincide, as was the case in 2010 when 5 Iyar corresponded to 19 April.
5 Resource Center for Palestinian Residency and Refugee Rights.
6 There has been some debate about whether Zochrot should start doing advocacy work in relation to the right of return alongside its educational activities on the Nakba (conference presentation by Zochrot director Liat Rosenberg, 2013).

3 Binationalism as settler decolonization? ICAHD and the One Democratic State

This chapter is based on Teodora Todorova, 'Reframing bi-nationalism in Palestine-Israel as a process of settler decolonisation', *Antipode*, 47 (5) (2015): 1367–87, DOI: 10.1111/anti.12153, reproduced with permission by John Wiley and Sons.

1 An institution of Israel's military government in the Occupied Palestinian Territories.
2 'No Home, No Homeland: A New Normative Framework for Examining the Practice of Administrative Home Demolitions in East Jerusalem'.

3 See Gordon (2013) for the Israeli High Court ruling against a petition for Israeli nationality.
4 The Law of Return (1950) makes it possible for every person defined as Jewish, anywhere in the world, to make aliyah, literally meaning 'ascent', to Israel and be granted automatic citizenship upon arrival in Israel.

4 Vulnerability as a politics of decolonial solidarity: The case of the Anarchists Against the Wall

This chapter is based on Teodora Todorova, 'Vulnerability as a politics of decolonial solidarity: The case of the Anarchists Against the Wall', *Identities*, 27 (3) (2019): 321–38, DOI: 10.1080/1070289X.2019.1647663, reprinted by permission of Taylor and Francis.

Bibliography

Abdo, Nahla. 2014. *Captive Revolution: Palestinian Women's Anti-colonial Struggle within the Israeli Prison System*. London: Pluto Press.

Abdo, Nahla, and Lentin, Ronit. 2004. *Women and the Politics of Military Confrontation: Palestinian and Israeli Gendered Narratives of Dislocation*. New York: Berghahn Books.

Abdo, Nahla, and Yuval-Davis, Nira. 1995. 'Palestine, Israel and the Zionist settler project'. In *Unsettling Settler Societies: Articulations of Gender, Race, Ethnicity, and Class*, edited by Daiva Stasiulis and Nira Yuval-Davis. London: Sage.

Abu-Lughod, Lila. 2007. 'Return to half-ruins: Memory, postmemory, and living history in Palestine'. In *Nakba: Palestine, 1948, and the Claims of Memory*, edited by Lila Abu-Lughod and Ahmad H. Sa'di. New York: Columbia University Press.

Abu-Lughod, Lila, and Sa'di, Ahmad H. (eds). 2007. *Nakba: Palestine, 1948, and the Claims of Memory*. New York: Columbia University Press.

Abunimah, Ali. 2006. *One Country: A Bold Proposal to End the Israeli-Palestinian Impasse*. New York: Metropolitan.

Abunimah, Ali. 2010. 'Reclaiming self-determination'. *Al-Shabaka Policy Brief*. https://al-shabaka.org/briefs/reclaiming-self-determination/.

Abunimah, Ali. 2012. 'ICAHD endorses one-state solution, warns against "warehousing" of Palestinians'. *Electronic Intifada*. 14 September. https://electronicintifada.net/blogs/ali-abunimah/icahd-endorses-one-state-solution-warns-against-warehousing-palestinians.

Abunimah, Ali. 2014. *The Battle for Justice in Palestine*. Chicago: Heymarket Books.

Abu-Saad, Ismael. 2019. 'Palestinian education in the Israeli settler state: Divide, rule and control'. *Settler Colonial Studies* 9 (1): 96–116. https://www.tandfonline.com/doi/abs/10.1080/2201473X.2018.1487125?journalCode=rset20.

Abu Zahra, Nadia. 2007. 'IDs and territory: Population control for resource expropriation'. In *War, Citizenship, Territory*, edited by Deborah Cowen and Emily Gilbert. New York: Routledge.

Adalah. 1998. 'Major findings of Adalah's report to the UN committee on the elimination of racial discrimination'. https://www.adalah.org/uploads/oldfiles/eng/intladvocacy/cerd-major-finding-march98.pdf.

Adalah. 2006. 'The future vision of the Palestinian Arabs in Israel'. https://www.adalah.org/uploads/oldfiles/newsletter/eng/dec06/tasawor-mostaqbali.pdf.

Bibliography

Adalah. 2011. 'Israeli human rights groups: The anti-boycott law harms freedom of expression and targets nonviolent political opposition to the Occupation'. https://www.adalah.org/uploads/oldfiles/upfiles/2011/12_July_2011_antiboycott.pdf.

Agamben, Giorgio. 1999. *Remnants of Auschwitz: The Witness and the Archive*. New York: Zone Books.

Agamben, Giorgio. 2005. *State of Exception*. Chicago: University of Chicago Press.

Aharonson, Ran. 1996. 'Settlement in Eretz Israel – a colonialist enterprise? "Critical" scholarship and historical geography'. *Israel Studies* 1 (2): 214–29. https://www.jstor.org/stable/30245498?seq=1.

AlJazeera. 2012. 'UN votes to upgrade Palestinian status'. 29 November. http://www.aljazeera.com/news/middleeast/2012/11/20121128142545792986.html.

AlJazeera. 2020. 'Egypt, France, Germany and Jordan warn Israel over annexation'. 7 July. https://www.aljazeera.com/news/2020/07/egypt-france-germany-jordan-warn-israel-annexation-200707183806305.html.

Allan, Diana K. 2007. 'The politics of witnessing: Remembering and forgetting 1948 in Shatila camp'. In *Nakba: Palestine, 1948, and the Claims of Memory*, edited by Lila Abu-Lughod and Ahmad H. Sa'di. New York: Columbia University Press.

Allen, Lori. 2018. 'What's in a link?: Transnational solidarities across Palestine and their intersectional possibilities'. *South Atlantic Quarterly* 117 (1): 111–33. https://doi.org/10.1215/00382876-4282064.

Allen, Theodore W. 2012. *The Invention of the White Race: The Origin of Racial Oppression in Anglo-America*. London: Verso.

Alsaafin, Linah. 2012. 'How obsession with "nonviolence" harms the Palestinian cause'. *Electronic Intifada*. 10 July. https://electronicintifada.net/content/how-obsession-nonviolence-harms-palestinian-cause/11482.

Al'sanah, Riya, and Ziadah, Rafeef. 2020. 'Of Course Israel exports arms and policing practices – it has spent decades "battle-testing" them on Palestinians'. *Novara Media*. 7 July. https://novaramedia.com/2020/07/07/of-course-israel-exports-arms-and-policing-practices-it-has-spent-decades-battle-testing-them-on-palestinians/.

Amir, Merav, and Kotef, Hagar. 2014. 'Limits of dissent, perils of activism: Spaces of resistance and the new security logic'. *Antipode: A Radical Journal of Geography* 47 (3): 671–88. https://onlinelibrary.wiley.com/doi/full/10.1111/anti.12130.

Amnesty International UK. 2011. 'Israel anti-boycott law an attack on freedom of expression'. 12 July. https://www.amnesty.org/en/press-releases/2011/07/israel-anti-boycott-law-attack-freedom-expression/.

Amnesty International UK. 2016. 'Israeli government must cease intimidation of human rights defenders, protect them from attacks'. 12 April. https://www.

amnestyusa.org/press-releases/israeli-government-must-cease-intimidation-of-human-rights-defenders-protect-them-from-attacks/.

Amnesty International UK. 2020a. 'USA / Israel and OPT: Dismal "peace deal" will only exacerbate violations'. 28 January. https://www.amnesty.org.uk/press-releases/usa-israel-and-opt-dismal-peace-deal-will-only-exacerbate-violations.

Amnesty International UK. 2020b. 'France: Landmark European Court of Human Rights judgment rules boycott campaign against Israel cannot be criminalised'. 11 June. https://www.amnesty.org.uk/press-releases/france-landmark-european-court-human-rights-judgment-rules-boycott-campaign-against.

Amrov, Sabrien. 2016. 'Why the divestment of G4S from Israel is a big deal'. *Middle East Monitor*. 11 March. https://www.middleeastmonitor.com/20160311-why-the-divestment-of-g4s-from-israel-is-a-big-deal/.

Anghie, Anthony. 2006. 'The evolution of international law: Colonial and postcolonial realities'. *Third World Quarterly* 27 (5): 739–53. https://www.jstor.org/stable/4017775?seq=1.

Anti-Blackness Roundtable. 2015. 'Roundtable on anti-Blackness and Black-Palestinian solidarity'. *Jadaliyya*. 3 June. https://www.jadaliyya.com/Details/32145.

Antonsich, Marco. 2010. 'Searching for belonging: An analytical framework'. *Geography Compass* 4 (6): 644–59. https://onlinelibrary.wiley.com/doi/10.1111/j.1749-8198.2009.00317.x.

Arendt, Hannah. [1951] 2017. *The Origins of Totalitarianism*. London: Penguin Books.

Arendt, Hannah. 2007. *The Jewish Writings*, edited by Jerome Kohn and Ron H. Feldman. New York: Schocken Books.

Arendt, Hannah. 1970. *On Violence*. London: Penguin Press.

Arendt, Hannah. 1958. *The Human Condition*. Chicago: University of Chicago Press.

Asseburg, Muriel. 2017. 'Shrinking spaces in Israel: Contraction of democratic space, consolidation of occupation, and ongoing human rights violations call for a pradigm [sic] shift in Europe's politics'. *Stiftung Wissenschaft und Politik*. https://nbn-resolving.org/urn:nbn:de:0168-ssoar-54348-3.

Assouline, Sarah. 2013. 'Here, murderers are heroes'. In *Anarchists Against the Wall*, edited by Uri Gordon and Ohal Grietzer. Oakland: AK Press.

Atran, Scot. 2010. *Talking to the Enemy: Violent Extremism, Sacred Values, and What It Means to Be Human*. London: Allen Lane.

Ayalon, Uri. 2004. 'Resisting the apartheid Wall'. *We Are All Anarchists Against the Wall!* http://www.fdca.it/fdcaen/press/pamphlets/waaaatw.htm.

Azoulay, Ariella, and Ophir, Adi. 2012. *The One-State Condition: Occupation and Democracy in Israel/Palestine*. Stanford, CA: Stanford University Press.

Barakat, Rana. 2018. 'Writing/righting Palestine studies: Settler colonialism, indigenous sovereignty and resisting the ghost(s) of history'. *Settler Colonial Studies* 8 (3): 349–63. https://www.tandfonline.com/doi/full/10.1080/2201473X.2017.1300048.

Barghouti, Omar. 2011. *Boycott, Divestment, Sanctions: The Global Struggle for Palestinian Rights*. London: Haymarket.

Barghouti, Omar. 2012. 'A secular democratic state in historic Palestine: Self-determination through ethical decolonisation'. In *After Zionism: One State for Israel and Palestine*, edited by Antony Loewenstein and Ahmed Moor. London: Saqi.

Bar-On, Dan. 2007. 'On the tense triangle between Germans, Israeli-Jews, and Palestinians'. In *Sedek: A Journal on the Ongoing Nakba Journal*. https://zochrot.org/en/sedek/50131.

Bar-On, Dan, and Sarsar, Saliba. 2004. 'Bridging the unbridgeable: The Holocaust and Al-Nakba'. *Palestine-Israel Journal of Politics, Economics and Culture* 11 (1): 63–70. https://pij.org/articles/17/bridging-the-unbridgeable-the-holocaust-and-alnakba.

BBC News. 2020. 'Johnson warns Israel against plans to annex part of West Bank'. 1 July. https://www.bbc.co.uk/news/world-middle-east-53248810.

BBC News. 2019. 'Extinction Rebellion: High Court rules London protest ban unlawful'. 6 November. https://www.bbc.co.uk/news/uk-50316561.

Beilin, Yossi. 2006. 'Just peace: A dangerous objective'. In *What Is a Just Peace*, edited by Pierre Allan and Alexis Keller. New York: Oxford University Press.

Beinart, Peter. 2020. 'I no longer believe in a Jewish State: For decades I argued for separation between Israelis and Palestinians. Now, I can imagine a Jewish home in an equal state'. *New York Times*. Opinion. 8 July. https://www.nytimes.com/2020/07/08/opinion/israel-annexation-two-state-solution.html.

Bell, Avril. 2009. 'Dilemmas of settler belonging: Roots, routes, and redemption in New Zealand national identity claims'. *Sociological Review* 57 (1): 145–62. https://journals.sagepub.com/doi/10.1111/j.1467-954X.2008.01808.x.

Bernstein, Deborah, and Swirski, Schlomo. 1982. 'The rapid economic development of Israel and the emergence of the ethnic division of labour'. *British Journal of Sociology* 33 (1): 64–85. https://www.jstor.org/stable/589337?seq=1.

Bhambra, Gurminder. 2016. 'Comparative historical sociology and the state: Problems of method'. *Cultural Sociology* 10 (3): 335–51. https://doi.org/10.1177/1749975516639085.

Bhandar, Brenna. 2018. *Colonial Lives of Property: Law, Land, and Racial Regimes of Ownership*. Durham: Duke University Press.

Bhandar, Brenna, and Ziadah, Rafeef. 2016. 'Acts and omissions: Framing settler colonialism in Palestine studies'. *Jadaliyya*, 14 January. http://www.jadaliyya.com/pages/index/23569/acts-and-omissions_framing-settler-colonialism-in.

Bisharat, George E. 1994. 'Land, law, and legitimacy in Israel and the Occupied Territories'. *American University Law Review* 43 (2): 467–561. https://digitalcommons.wcl.american.edu/aulr/vol43/iss2/3/.

Bisharat, George E. 2008. 'Maximizing rights: The one state solution to the Palestinian-Israeli conflict'. *Global Jurist* 8 (2): 1–36. https://www.degruyter.com/view/journals/gj/8/2/article-gj.2008.8.2.1266.xml.xml.

Boehm, Omri. 2020. 'After liberal Zionism, the one hope for a democratic Israel'. *New York Review of Books*. 9 June. https://www.nybooks.com/daily/2020/06/09/after-liberal-zionism-the-one-hope-for-a-democratic-israel/.

Bot, Michiel. 2019. 'The right to boycott: BDS, law, and politics in a global context'. *Transnational Legal Theory* 10 (3–4): 421–45. https://doi.org/10.1080/20414005.2019.1672134.

Bouattia, Malia. 2018. 'Students not suspects: Prevent on campus'. *New Arab*. 13 April. https://www.alaraby.co.uk/english/comment/2018/4/13/students-not-suspects-prevent-on-campus.

Bouattia, Malia. 2019. 'Warwick Occupy: How students can fight back to reclaim free speech'. *Middle East Eye*. 6 December. https://www.middleeasteye.net/opinion/warwick-occupy-how-students-can-fight-back-reclaim-free-speech.

Boudreau Morris, Katie. 2017. 'Decolonizing solidarity: Cultivating relationships of discomfort'. *Settler Colonial Studies* 7 (4): 456–73. https://www.tandfonline.com/doi/abs/10.1080/2201473X.2016.1241210.

Brown, Wendy. 2010. *Walled States, Waning Sovereignty*. New York: Zone Books.

Bruyneel, Kevin. 2019. 'The BDS movement, political theory, and settler memory'. *Contemporary Political Theory* 18 (3): 452–6. https://link.springer.com/article/10.1057/s41296-019-00331-1.

B'Tselem. 2017. 'Planning Policy in the West Bank'. 11 November. https://www.btselem.org/planning_and_building.

Burnat, Emad, and Davidi, Guy (directors). 2011. *5 Broken Cameras*. Israel/Palestine: New Wave Films.

Busbridge, Rachel. 2018. 'Israel-Palestine and the settler colonial "turn": From interpretation to decolonization'. *Theory, Culture, Society* 35 (1): 91–115. https://journals.sagepub.com/doi/10.1177/0263276416688544.

Butler, Judith. 1997. *The Psychic Life of Power: Theories in Subjection*. Stanford, CA: Stanford University Press.

Butler, Judith. 2004. *Precarious Life: The Powers of Mourning and Violence.* London: Verso.

Butler, Judith. 2008. 'An account of oneself'. In *Judith Butler in Conversation: Analyzing the Texts and Talks of Everyday Life*, edited by Bronwyn Davies. London: Routledge.

Butler, Judith. 2009. *Frames of War: When Is Life Grievable?* London: Verso.

Butler, Judith. 2012. *Parting Ways: Jewishness and the Critique of Zionism.* New York: Columbia University Press.

Butler, Judith. 2015. *Notes Towards a Performative Theory of Assembly.* Cambridge, MA: Harvard University Press.

Butler, Judith. 2016. 'Vulnerability and resistance'. In *Vulnerability in Resistance*, edited by Judith Butler, Zeynep Gambetti and Leticia Sabsay. Durham: Duke University Press.

Buttigieg, Joseph A. 1995. 'Gramsci on civil society'. *Boundary 2* 22 (3): 1–32. https://www.jstor.org/stable/303721?seq=1#metadata_info_tab_contents.

Buttigieg, Joseph A. 2005. 'The contemporary discourse on civil society: A Gramscian critique'. *Boundary 2* 32 (1): 32–52. https://read.dukeupress.edu/boundary-2/article-abstract/32/1/33/6222/The-Contemporary-Discourse-on-Civil-Society-A?redirectedFrom=fulltext.

Carrillo Rowe A. 2005. 'Be longing: Toward a feminist politics of relation'. *NWSA Journal* 17 (2): 15–37. https://www.jstor.org/stable/pdf/4317124.pdf?seq=1.

Carter Hallward, Maia, and Norman, Julie M. (eds). 2011. *Nonviolent Resistance in the Second Intifada: Activism and Advocacy.* Basingstoke: Palgrave Macmillan.

Center for Constitutional Rights. 2015. 'The Palestine exception to free speech: A movement under attack in the US'. https://ccrjustice.org/the-palestine-exception.

Central Bureau of Statistics. 2009. 'Israel in figures 2009'. https://old.cbs.gov.il/publications/isr_in_n09e.pdf.

Chetrit, Sami Shalom. 2010. *Intra-Jewish Conflict in Israel: White Jews, Black Jews.* London: Routledge.

Clark, Howard. 2009. *People Power: Unarmed Resistance and Global Solidarity.* London: Pluto Press.

Clarno, Andy. 2017. *Neoliberal Apartheid: Palestine-Israel and South Africa After 1994.* Chicago: University of Chicago Press.

Cockburn, Cynthia. 2012. *Anti-Militarism: Political and Gender Dynamics of Peace Movements.* London: Palgrave Macmillan.

Cocks, Joan. 2006. 'Jewish nationalism and the question of Palestine'. *Interventions* 8 (1): 24–39.

Cohen, Stanley. 2001. *States of Denial: Knowing about Atrocities and Suffering*. Cambridge: Polity Press.

Collins, John. 2011. *Global Palestine*. London: Hurst.

Dalla Negra, Cecilia. 2012. '"I can't dictate methods of Palestinian struggle": Israeli boycott activist interviewed'. *Electronic Intifada*. 8 August. https://electronicintifada.net/content/i-cant-dictate-methods-palestinian-struggle-israeli-boycott-activist-interviewed/11561.

Darweish, Marwan, and Rigby, Andrew. 2015. *Popular Protest in Palestine: The Uncertain Future of Unarmed Resistance*. London: Pluto Press.

Davies, Rochelle. 2007. 'Mapping the past, re-creating the homeland: Memories of village places in pre-1948 Palestine'. In *Nakba: Palestine, 1948, and the Claims of Memory*, edited by Lila Abu-Lughod and Ahmad H. Sa'di. New York: Columbia University Press.

Davis, Uri. [1987] 1990. *Israel, an Apartheid State*. London: Zed Books.

Davis, Uri. 2003. *Apartheid Israel: Possibilities for the Struggle Within*. London: Zed Books.

Davis, Uri. 2010. 'Naming the coloniser in geographic Palestine: Conceptual and political double binds and their possible solutions'. In *Across the Wall: Narratives of Israeli-Palestinian History*, edited by Jamil Hilal and Ilan Pappé. London: I.B. Tauris.

Day, Iyko. 2015. 'Being or nothingness: Indigeneity, antiblackness, and settler colonial critique'. *Critical Ethnic Studies* 1 (2): 102–21. https://www.jstor.org/stable/pdf/10.5749/jcritethnstud.1.2.0102.pdf?seq=1.

Dayan, Hilla. 2019. 'Neozionism: portrait of a contemporary hegemony'. *Settler Colonial Studies* 9 (1): 22–40. https://www.tandfonline.com/doi/full/10.1080/2201473X.2018.1487117.

Dean, Jodi. 2019. 'BDS and international solidarity'. *Contemporary Political Theory* 18 (3): 459–64. https://doi.org/10.1057/s41296-019-00331-1.

Dor, Daniel. 2005. *The Suppression of Guilt: The Israeli Media and the Re-Occupation of the West Bank*. London: Pluto Press.

Dudouet, Veronique. 2009. 'Cross-border nonviolent advocacy during the Second Palestinian Intifada: The International Solidarity Movement'. In *People Power: Unarmed Resistance and Global Solidarity*, edited by Howard Clark. London: Pluto Press.

Duffield, Mark. 2001. *Global Governance and the New Wars: The Merging of Development and Security*. London: Zed Books.

Duffield, Mark. 2007. *Unending War: Governing the World of Peoples*. Cambridge: Polity Press.

Eastwood, James. 2017. *Ethics as a Weapon of War: Militarism and Morality in Israel*. Cambridge: Cambridge University Press.

Edmonds, Ruth. 2013. 'Hey babe, hope you're not in jail'. In *Anarchists Against The Wall*, edited by Uri Gordon and Ohal Grietzer. Oakland: AK Press.

Eldar, Akiva, and Zertal, Idith. 2007. *Lords of the Land: The War over Israel's Settlements in the Occupied Territories, 1967–2007*. New York: Nation Books.

Elia, Nada. 2012. 'Gay rights with a side of apartheid'. *Settler Colonial Studies* 2 (2): 49–68. https://www.tandfonline.com/doi/abs/10.1080/2201473X.2012.10648841.

Elkins, Caroline, and Pedersen Susan (eds). 2005. *Settler Colonialism in the Twentieth Century*. London: Routledge.

Erakat, Noura. 2015. 'Whiteness as property in Israel: Revival, rehabilitation, and removal'. *Harvard Journal on Racial and Ethnic Justice*. https://papers.ssrn.com/sol3/papers.cfm?abstract_id=2626870.

Erakat, Noura. 2019. *Justice for Some: Law and the Question of Palestine*. Stanford, CA: Stanford University Press.

Estes, Nick. 2019. *Our History is the Future: Standing Rock versus the Dakota Access Pipeline, and the Long Tradition of Indigenous Resistance*. London: Verso.

European Legal Support Centre. 2020. https://elsc.support/?i=1.

Farsakh, Leila. 2011. 'The one-state solution and the Israeli-Palestinian conflict: Palestinian challenges and prospects'. *Middle Eastern Journal* 65 (1): 55–71. https://www.jstor.org/stable/23012093?seq=1.

Feinstein, Yuval, and Ben-Eliezer, Uri. 2007. ' "The Battle over Our Homes": Reconstructing/deconstructing sovereign practices around Israel's separation barrier on the West Bank'. *Israel Studies* 12 (1): 172–92. https://www.jstor.org/stable/30245812?seq=1.

Feldman, Jackie. 2007. 'Between Yad Vashem and Mt. Herzl: Changing inscriptions of sacrifice on Jerusalem's "Mountain of Memory" '. *Anthropological Quarterly* 80 (4): 1147–74. https://www.jstor.org/stable/pdf/30052776.pdf?seq=1.

Fernandez, Johanna. 2017. 'Structures of settler colonial domination in Israel and in the United States'. *Decolonization: Indigeneity, Education & Society* 6 (1): 29–44. https://jps.library.utoronto.ca/index.php/des/article/view/28901.

Fiala, Andrew. 2010. *Public War, Private Conscience: The Ethic of Political Violence*. London: Continuum International.

Filc, Dani. 2018. 'Political radicalization in Israel: From a populist habitus to radical right populism in government'. In *Expressions of Radicalization*, edited by Kristian Steiner and Andreas Önnerfors. London: Palgrave Macmillan, Cham.

Foundation for Middle East Peace. 2012. 'Comprehensive settlement population 1972–2011.' 13 January. https://fmep.org/resource/comprehensive-settlement-population-1972-2010/.

Free Speech on Israel. 2017. 'Counsel's opinion on the IHRA definition'. *Free Speech on Israel*. https://freespeechonisrael.org.uk/ihra-opinion/#sthash.cE9aFaD0.SBwQbLj4.dpbs.

Gal, Daniel. 2017. 'The challenges of an ethnic-democracy: Populism, Netanyahu and Israel's path'. *Democracy and Resentment* 3: 1–18. https://doi.org/10.26481/marble.2017.v3.555.

Gayle, Damien. 2019. 'Police ban Extinction Rebellion protests from whole of London'. 14 October. https://www.theguardian.com/environment/2019/oct/14/police-ban-extinction-rebellion-protests-from-whole-of-london.

Ghanim, Honaida. 2008. 'Thanatopolitics: The case of the colonial occupation of Palestine'. In *Thinking Palestine*, edited by Ronit Lentin. London: Zed Books.

Goldberg, David Theo. 2002. *The Racial State*. Oxford: Blackwell.

Goldstein, Alyosha, and Lubin, Alex (eds). 2008. *Settler Colonialism*. Durham: Duke University Press.

Goodstein. Laurie. 2017. 'New Israel law bars foreign critics from entering the country'. 7 March. *New York Times*. https://www.nytimes.com/2017/03/07/world/middleeast/israel-knesset-vote-boycott-bds-reform-judaism.html.

Gordon, Neve. 2008. 'From colonisation to separation: Exploring the structure of Israel's occupation'. *Third World Quarterly* 29 (1): 25–44. https://www.tandfonline.com/doi/abs/10.1080/01436590701726442.

Gordon, Neve. 2013. 'High court rules: It is impossible to be Israeli'. *AlJazeera*. 21 October. https://www.aljazeera.com/opinions/2013/10/21/high-court-rules-it-is-impossible-to-be-israeli.

Gordon, Neve. 2014. 'Human rights as a security threat: Lawfare and the campaign against human rights NGOs'. *Law and Society Review* 48 (2): 311–44. https://onlinelibrary.wiley.com/doi/abs/10.1111/lasr.12074.

Gordon, Neve, and Perugini, Nicola. 2016. 'The politics of human shielding: On the resignification of space and the constitution of civilians as shields in liberal wars'. *Environment and Planning D: Society and Space* 34 (1): 168–87. https://journals.sagepub.com/doi/full/10.1177/0263775815607478.

Gordon, Uri. 2008. *Anarchy Alive! Anti-Authoritarian Politics from Practice to Theory*. London: Pluto Press.

Gordon, Uri. 2010. 'Against the Wall: Anarchist mobilization in the Israeli–Palestinian Conflict'. *Peace and Change* 35 (3): 412–33. https://doi.org/10.1111/j.1468-0130.2010.00641.x.

Gordon, Uri. 2016. 'Anarchism and multiculturalism'. In *Philosophies of Multiculturalism: Beyond Liberalism*, edited by Luis Cordeiro-Rodrigues and Marko Simendic. Abingdon: Routledge.

Gordon, Uri, and Grietzer Ohal (eds). 2013. *Anarchists Against the Wall*. Oakland: AK Press.

Gramsci, Antonio. 1992. *Prison Notebooks*, edited with introduction by Joseph A. Buttigieg, translated by Joseph A. Buttigieg and Antonio Callari. New York: Columbia University Press.

Gregory, Derek. 2004. *The Colonial Present: Afghanistan, Palestine, Iraq*. Oxford: Blackwell.

Grinberg, Lev. 2004. 'Post-mortem for the Ashkenazi left'. In *Who's Left in Israel: Radical Political Alternatives for the Future of Israel*, edited by Dan Leon. Brighton: Sussex University Press.

Haddad, Touffic. 2016. *Palestine Ltd: Neoliberalism and Nationalism in the Occupied Territories*. London: I.B. Tauris.

Halper, Jeff. 2010. *An Israeli in Palestine Second Edition: Resisting Dispossession Redeeming Israel*. London: Pluto Press.

Halper, Jeff. 2012. 'Beyond regional peace to global reality'. In *After Zionism: One State for Israel and Palestine*, edited by Antony Loewenstein and Ahmed Moor. London: Saqi.

Halper, Jeff. 2013. 'Towards an end-game in Palestine-Israel – while imagining the future'. https://icahd.org/2013/04/12/a-report-of-the-icahd-uk-conference/.

Halper, Jeff, and Epshtain, Itay. 2012. 'In the name of justice: Key issues around a single state'. 13 September. https://icahd.org/2019/05/24/in-the-name-of-justice-key-issues-around-a-single-state-2/.

Hammami, Rema. 2016. 'Precarious politics: The activism of "bodies that count" (aligning with those that don't) in Palestine's colonial frontier'. In *Vulnerability in Resistance*, edited by Judith Butler, Zeynep Gambetti and Leticia Sabsay. Durham: Duke University Press.

Hanafi, Sari. 2009. 'Spacio-cide: Colonial politics, invisibility, and rezoning in Palestinian Territory'. *Contemporary Arab Affairs* 2 (1): 106–21. https://www.tandfonline.com/doi/abs/10.1080/17550910802622645?scroll=top&needAccess=true&journalCode=rcaa20.

Harvey, David. 2009. *Cosmopolitanism and the Geographies of Freedom*. New York: Columbia University Press.

Hass, Amira. 2002. 'Always a fighter, always a terrorist'. *ZNet*. 9 October. https://zcomm.org/znetarticle/always-a-fighter-always-a-terrorist-by-amira-hass/.

Hawari, Yara, Plonski, Sharri, and Weizman, Elian. 2019. 'Seeing Israel through Palestine: Knowledge production as anti-colonial praxis'. *Settler*

Colonial Studies 9 (1): 155–75. https://www.tandfonline.com/doi/abs/10.1080/2201473X.2018.1487129?journalCode=rset20.

Hermann, Tamar. 2005. 'The bi-national idea in Israel/Palestine: Past and present'. *Nations and Nationalism* 11 (3): 381–401. https://doi.org/10.1111/j.1354-5078.2005.00210.x.

Hever, Shir. 2010. *The Political Economy of Israel's Occupation: Repression Beyond Exploitation*. London: Pluto Press.

Hever. Shir. 2019. 'The nightwatchman becomes a mercenary'. *Settler Colonial Studies* 9 (1): 78–95. https://doi.org/10.1080/2201473X.2018.1487124.

Hilal, Jamil (ed.). 2007. *Where Now for Palestine? The Demise of the Two-State Solution*. London: Zed Books.

Hilsum, Lindsay. 2001. 'The death of the Israeli left'. *New Statesman*. 5 February. https://www.newstatesman.com/node/193886.

Hirsch, Marianne. 1997. *Family Frames: Photography, Narrative and Post-Memory*. Cambridge, MA: Harvard University Press.

Human Rights Watch. 2019. 'Israel expels human rights watch director today: Group will keep documenting abuses by all parties'. 25 November. https://www.hrw.org/news/2019/11/25/israel-expels-human-rights-watch-director-today.

Human Rights Watch. 2011. 'Israel: Anti-boycott bill stifles expression: Penalties could cause human rights groups to shut down'. 13 July. http://www.hrw.org/en/news/2011/07/13/israel-anti-boycott-bill-stifles-expression.

Hyndman, Jennifer. 2005. 'Feminist geopolitics revisited: Body counts in Iraq'. *Professional Geographer* 59 (1): 35–46. https://doi.org/10.1111/j.1467-9272.2007.00589.x.

ICAHD. 2005. 'ICAHD First Israeli Peace Group to call for Sanctions'. 27 January. https://icahd.org/2019/05/24/icahd-first-israeli-peace-group-to-call-for-sanctions/amp/.

ICAHD. 2006. 'Jeff Halper Nominated for Nobel Peace Prize 2006'. https://icahd.org/2006/04/15/jeff-halper-nominated-for-nobel-peace-prize-2006/.

ICAHD. 2012a. 'Information for the adoption of a list of issues for Israel before the human rights committee (ICCPR)'. https://tbinternet.ohchr.org/Treaties/CCPR/Shared%20Documents/ISR/INT_CCPR_NGO_ISR_105_9105_E.pdf.

ICAHD. 2021. 'Boycotts, Divestments, and Sanctions'. https://icahd.org/get-the-facts/boycotts-divestments-sanctions/.

Im Tirtzu. 2011. 'Politicization at Ben Gurion University'. http://imti.org.il/wp-content/uploads/2015/09/%D7%90%D7%A0%D7%92%D7%9C%D7%99%D7%AA-%D7%A1%D7%95%D7%A4%D7%99.pdf.

Institute for Palestine Studies. 1991. 'A survey of Palestine, prepared in December 1945 and January 1946 for the information of the Anglo-American Committee of Inquiry'. Washington, DC: Institute for Palestine Studies.

International Holocaust Remembrance Alliance. 2018. 'Working definition of antisemitism'. https://www.holocaustremembrance.com/working-definition-antisemitism.

Jackson, Jack. 2019. 'BDS, political theory, and US constitutional law'. *Contemporary Political Theory* 18 (3): 464–8. https://doi.org/10.1057/s41296-019-00331-1.

Jamal, Amal. 2018. 'The rise of "bad civil society" in Israel: Nationalist civil society organizations and the politics of delegitimization'. *Stiftung Wissenschaft und Politik*. https://nbn-resolving.org/urn:nbn:de:0168-ssoar-56079-4.

Jamal, Amal. 2019. 'Neo-Zionism and Palestine: The unveiling of setter colonial practices in mainstream Zionism'. *Journal of Holy Land and Palestine Studies* 16 (1): 47–78. https://doi.org/10.1111/j.1467-9272.2007.00589.x.

Jawad, Rania. 2011. 'Staging resistance in Bil'in: The performance of violence in a Palestinian village'. *Drama Review* 55 (4): 128–43. https://www.mitpressjournals.org/doi/10.1162/DRAM_a_00127.

Kaldor, Mary. 2003. *Global Civil Society: An Answer to War*. Cambridge: Polity Press.

Kamel, Lorenzo. 2014. 'Overcoming post-colonialism in the Eastern Mediterranean'. Paper presented at the British Society for Middle Eastern Studies Annual Conference.

Karatzogianni, Athina, and Robinson, Andrew. 2010. *Power, Resistance and Conflict in the Contemporary World: Social Movements, Networks and Hierarchies*. London: Routledge.

Karsh, Efraim. 2012. 'Special issue – war by other means: Israel and its detractors'. *Israel Affairs* 18 (3): 319–501. https://www.tandfonline.com/doi/abs/10.1080/13537121.2012.689521.

Kaufman-Lacusta, Maxine. 2010. *Refusing to Be Enemies: Palestinian and Israeli Nonviolent Resistance to the Occupation*. Washington, DC: Ithaca Press.

Keck, Margaret E., and Sikkink, Kathryn. 1998. *Activists Beyond Borders: Advocacy Networks in International Politics*. London: Cornell University Press.

Keidar, Roy, and Shayshon, Eran. 2011. 'The boycott law plays to the hands of de-legitimizers'. http://www.reut-institute.org/en/Publication.aspx?PublicationId=4044.

Khalidi, Rashid. 1997. *Palestinian Identity: The Construction of Modern National Consciousness*. New York: Columbia University Press.

Khalidi, Rashid. 2006. *The Iron Cage: The Story of the Palestinian Struggle for Statehood*. Oxford: Oneworld.

Khalidi, Walid. 1992. *All That Remains: The Palestinian Villages Occupied and Depopulated by Israel in 1948*. Washington, DC: Institute for Palestine Studies.

Khalidi, Walid. [1959] 2005. '"Why did the Palestinians leave revisited", 2005'. *Journal of Palestine Studies* 34 (2): 42–54.

Khoury, Jack, and Lis, Jonathan. 2011. 'Knesset passes two bills slammed as discriminatory by rights groups'. *Ha'aretz*. 24 March. http://www.haaretz.com/print-edition/ news/knesset-passes-two-bills-slammed-as-discriminatory-by-rights-groups-1.351462.

Khoury-Bisharat, H. 2019. 'The unintended consequences of the goldstone commission of inquiry on human rights organizations in Israel'. *European Journal of International Law* 3 (3): 877–901. https://academic.oup.com/ejil/article-abstract/30/3/877/5673331?redirectedFrom=fulltext.

Kidron, Peretz (ed.). 2004. *Refusnik!: Israel's Soldiers of Conscience*. London: Zed Books.

Kifukwe, Gwamaka. 2011. 'Geographies of development expertise in Tanzania, 1992–2007'. Doctoral Thesis. University of Nottingham.

Kilroy, Eleanor. 2011. 'Interview with Israeli BDS activist Tali Shapiro: The fear of international isolation is shifting the discourse in Israel'. *Mondoweiss*. 29 March. https://mondoweiss.net/2011/03/interview-with-israeli-bds-activist-tali-shapiro-the-fear-of-international-isolation-is-shifting-the-discourse-in-israel/.

Kite, Harry, Salvoni, Nell, and Kinder, Emily. 2019. 'Sociology students release open letter in solidarity with professor accused of antisemitism'. *The Boar*. https://theboar.org/2019/11/sociology-students-release-open-letter-in-solidarity-with-professor-accused-of-antisemitism/.

Klein, Naomi. 2007. *The Shock Doctrine: The Rise of Disaster Capitalism*. London: Penguin Books.

Knesset. 'The Law of Return 5710 (1950)'. https://www.knesset.gov.il/laws/special/eng/return.htm.

Knesset. 'Nationality Law 5712 (1952)'. https://www.knesset.gov.il/review/data/eng/law/kns2_nationality_eng.pdf.

Knesset. 2018. 'Basic Law: Israel - The Nation State of the Jewish People'. https://knesset.gov.il/laws/special/eng/BasicLawNationState.pdf.

Kook, Rebecca. 2017. 'Representation, minorities and electoral reform: The case of the Palestinian minority in Israel'. *Ethnic and Racial Studies* 40 (12): 2039–57. https://doi.org/10.1080/01419870.2017.1277027.

Koopman, Sara. 2008. 'Imperialism within: Can the master's tools bring down empire?' *ACME: An International Journal for Critical Geographies* 7 (2): 283–307. https://acme-journal.org/index.php/acme/article/view/807.

Krebs, Mike, and Olwan, Dana M. 2012. '"From Jerusalem to the Grand River, Our Struggles are One": Challenging Canadian and Israeli settler colonialism'. *Settler Colonial Studies* 2 (2): 138–64. https://doi.org/10.1080/2201473X.2012.10648846.

Kurasawa, Fuyuki. 2004. 'A cosmopolitanism from below: Alternative globalisation and the creation of a solidarity without bounds'. *European Journal of Sociology* 45 (2): 233–55. https://www.jstor.org/stable/23999133?seq=1.

Lahav, Hagar. 2010. 'The giver of life and the griever of death: Women in the Israeli TV coverage of the Second Lebanon War (2006)'. *Communication, Culture & Critique* 3 (2): 242–69. https://onlinelibrary.wiley.com/doi/abs/10.1111/j.1753-9137.2010.01069.x.

Lamarche, Karine. 2019. 'The backlash against Israeli human rights NGOs, grounds, players, and implications'. *International Journal of Politics, Culture, and Society* 32: 301–22. https://doi.org/10.1007/s10767-018-9312-z.

Land, Clare. 2015. *Decolonizing Solidarity: Dilemmas and Directions for Supporters of Indigenous Struggles*. London: Zed Books.

Landau, Noa. 2018. 'Israel publishes BDS blacklist: These are the 20 groups whose members will be denied entry'. *Ha'aretz*. 7 January. https://www.haaretz.com/israel-news/israel-publishes-bds-blacklist-these-20-groups-will-be-denied-entry-1.5729880.

Lavie, Smadar. [2014] 2018. *Wrapped in the Flag of Israel: Mizrahi Single Mothers and Bureaucratic Torture*. Lincoln: University of Nebraska Press.

Lemish, Dafna. 2005. 'Guest editor's introduction'. *Feminist Media Studies* 5 (3): 275–80.

Lentin, Ronit (ed.). 2008. 'The contested memory of dispossession: Commemorizing the Palestinian Nakba in Israel'. *Thinking Palestine*. London: Zed Books.

Lentin, Ronit. 2018. *Traces of Racial Exception: Racializing Israeli Settler Colonialism*. London: Bloomsbury.

Levinson, Chaim. 2009. 'IDF: More than 300,000 settlers live in West Bank'. *Ha'aretz*. 7 July. http://www.haaretz.com/print-edition/news/idf-more-than-300-000-settlers-livein-westbank-1.280778.

Levy, Yagil, Lomsky-Feder, Edna, and Harel, Noa. 2010. 'From "Obligatory Militarism" to "Contractual Militarism" – competing models of citizenship'. In *Militarism and Israeli Society*, edited by Gabriel Sheffer and Barak Oren. Bloomington: Indiana University Press.

Lintl, Peter. 2016. 'The dynamics of a right-wing coalition: How the failure of the peace process encourages domestic populism in Israel'. *Stiftung Wissenschaft und Politik*. https://nbn-resolving.org/urn:nbn:de:0168-ssoar-48905-0.

Lis, Jonathan. 2011. 'Israel passes law banning call for boycott. *Ha'aretz*. 11 July. https://www.haaretz.com/1.5026309.

Lis, Jonathan. 2014. 'Netanyahu's cabinet approves controversial bill enshrining Israel as Jewish nation-state'. *Ha'aretz*. 23 November. http://www.haaretz.com/news/national/1.628001.

Lloyd, David. 2012. 'Settler colonialism and the state of exception: The example of Palestine/Israel'. *Settler Colonial Studies* 2 (1): 59–80. https://doi.org/10.1080/2201473X.2012.10648826.

Loewenstein, Antony, and Moor, Ahmed (eds). 2012. *After Zionism: One State for Israel and Palestine*. London: Saqi.

Long, Joanna C. 2006. 'Border anxiety in Palestine-Israel'. *Antipode* 38 (1): 107–27. https://onlinelibrary.wiley.com/doi/abs/10.1111/j.0066-4812.2006.00567.x.

Macoun, Alissa, and Strakosch, Elizabeth. 2013. 'The ethical demands of settler colonial theory'. *Settler Colonial Studies* 3 (3–4): 426–43. https://doi.org/10.1080/2201473X.2013.810695.

Mada Al-Carmel. 2007. 'The Haifa Declaration'. https://mada-research.org/wp-content/uploads/2007/09/watheeqat-haifa-english.pdf.

Mahrouse, Ghada. 2014. *Conflicted Commitments: Race, Privilege, and Power in Transnational Activism*. London: McGill-Queen's University Press.

Mamdani, Mahmood. 2002. 'Amnesty or impunity: A preliminary critique of the report of the Truth and Reconciliation Commission of South Africa (TRC)'. *Diacritics* 32 (3–4): 32–59. https://www.jstor.org/stable/1566444?seq=1.

Mansdorf, Irvin J. 2010. 'Is Israel a colonial state? The political psychology of Palestinian nomenclature'. *Jerusalem Centre for Public Affairs*. https://jcpa.org/article/is-israel-a-colonial-state-the-political-psychology-of-palestinian-nomenclature/.

Masalha, Nur. 2003. *The Politics of Denial: Israel and the Palestinian Refugee Problem*. London: Pluto Press.

Masalha, Nur. 2005. *Catastrophe Remembered: Palestine, Israel and the Internal Refugees: Essays in Memory of Edward W. Said (1935–2003)*. London: Zed Books.

Masalha, Nur. 2012. *The Palestine Nakba: Decolonising History, Narrating the Subaltern, Reclaiming Memory*. London: Zed Books.

Massad, Joseph. 1996. 'Zionism's internal others: Israel and the oriental Jews'. *Journal of Palestine Studies* 25 (4): 53–68. https://www.jstor.org/stable/2538006.

Mavroudi, Elizabeth. 2010. 'Imagining a shared state in Palestine-Israel'. *Antipode* 42 (1): 152–78. https://onlinelibrary.wiley.com/doi/abs/10.1111/j.1467-8330.2009.00735.x.

Mayer, Tamar. 2008. 'Nation and gender in Jewish Israel'. In *War, Citizenship and Territory*, edited by Deborah Cowen and Emily Gilbert. London: Routledge.

Mbembe, J. Achille. 2003. 'Necropolitics'. *Public Culture* 15 (1): 11–40. https://muse.jhu.edu/article/39984.

McVeigh, Karen. 2015. 'NUS fights back against government's "chilling" counter-radicalisation strategy'. 2 September. https://www.theguardian.com/education/2015/sep/02/nus-fights-back-against-governments-chilling-counter-radicalisation-strategy.

Mercer, Claire. 2002. 'NGOs, civil society and democratization: A critical review of the literature'. *Progress in Development Studies* 2 (5): 5–22. https://doi.org/10.1191/ 1464993402ps027ra.

Middle East Eye. 2020. ' "Apartheid": US Jewish groups reject Trump's Israel-Palestine plan'. 28 January. https://www.middleeasteye.net/news/anti-occupation-us-jewish-groups-reject-trumps-middle-east-plan.

Middle East Monitor. 2020. 'University backs lecturer on "free speech" grounds following alleged anti-Semitism complaint'. 4 September. https://www.middleeastmonitor.com/20200904-university-backs-lecturer-on-free-speech-grounds-following-alleged-anti-semitism-complaint/.

Middle East Monitor. 2018. 'New Israel report exposes role of NGO monitor in defaming rights activists'. 1 October. http://www.middleeastmonitor.com/20181001-new-israel-report-exposes-role-of-ngo-monitor-in-defaming-rights-activists/.

Mills, Catherine. 2003. 'An ethics of bare life: Agamben on witnessing'. *Borderlands* 2 (1). https://research.monash.edu/en/publications/an-ethics-of-bare-life-agamben-on-witnessing-review-essay-of-gior.

Misgav, Chen. 2013. 'Another land'. *Anarchists Against the Wall*, edited by Uri Gordon and Ohal Grietzer. Oakland: AK Press.

Morgensen, Scott Lauria. 2012. 'Queer settler colonialism in Canada and Israel: Articulating two-spirit and Palestinian queer critiques'. *Settler Colonial Studies* 2 (2): 67–189. https://doi.org/10.1080/2201473X.2012.10648848.

Morgensen, Scott Lauria. 2014. 'White settlers and indigenous solidarity: Confronting white supremacy, answering decolonial alliances'. *Decolonization: Indigeneity, Education & Society*. https://decolonization.wordpress.com/2014/05/26/white-settlers-and-indigenous-solidarity-confronting-white-supremacy-answering-decolonial-alliances/.

Morrar, Ayed. 2010. 'Not just a friend: One Palestinian's view of Israeli activist Jonathan Pollak'. *Huffington Post*. 29 December. https://www.huffingtonpost.com/ayedmorrar/not-just-a-friend-one-pal_b_802468.html.

Morris, Benny. [1987] 2004. *The Birth of the Palestinian Refugee Problem, 1947–49 Revisited*. Cambridge: Cambridge University Press.

Moreton-Robinson, Aileen. 2015. *The White Possessive: Property, Power and Indigenous Sovereignty*. London: University of Minnesota Press.

Musih, Norma, and Bronstein, Eitan. 2010. 'Thinking practically about the return of the Palestinian refugees'. *Sedek: A Journal on the Ongoing Nakba*. http://zochrot.org/en/sedek/56234.

Nagdee, Ilyas. 2019. 'Reforming the prevent strategy won't work. It must be abolished'. *The Guardian*. 9 October. https://www.theguardian.com/commentisfree/2019/oct/09/prevent-strategy-abolished-secret-counter-terror-database.

Nakata, N. Martin, et al. 2012. 'Decolonial goals and pedagogies for indigenous studies'. *Decolonization: Indigeneity, Education & Society* 1 (1): 120–40. https://jps.library.utoronto.ca/index.php/des/article/view/18628.

Nash, Kate. 2009. 'Between citizenship and human rights'. *Sociology* 43 (6): 1067–83. https://doi.org/10.1177/0038038509345702.

Nashif, Nadim, and Naamneh, Raya. 2016. 'Palestinian citizens in Israel: A fast-shrinking civic space'. *Al-Shabaka: The Palestinian Policy Network*. https://al-shabaka.org/wp-content/uploads/2016/01/Nashif_Naamneh_Commentary_Eng_Jan2016.pdf.

NGO Monitor. 2008. 'Press release: Following NGO monitor reports, European Union ends ICAHD funding'. 11 September. http://bit.ly/1ORKeKW.

Norman, Julie M. 2010. *The Second Palestinian Intifada: Civil Resistance*. London: Routledge.

OCHAOPT. 2018. 'West Bank barrier'. https://www.ochaopt.org/theme/west-bank-barrier.

Olwan, Dana M. 2019. 'Feminist political solidarity and the BDS movement'. *Contemporary Political Theory* 18 (3): 456–9. https://doi.org/10.1057/s41296-019-00331-1.

One Democratic State Campaign. 2020. https://onestatecampaign.org/en/.

Owen, David S., and Strong, Tracy B. (eds). 2004. *Max Weber: The Vocation Lectures*. Indianapolis, IN: Hackett.

Palestinian Return Centre. 2018. 'Syria's Palestinian refugees: An account of violence, precarious existence and uncertain futures'. https://prc.org.uk/upload/library/files/SyriasPalestinianRefugeesAccOfViolence.pdf.

Pallister-Wilkins, Polly. 2009. 'Radical ground: Israeli and Palestinian activists and joint protest against the Wall'. *Social Movement Studies* 8 (4): 393–407. https://www.tandfonline.com/doi/abs/10.1080/14742830903234262.

Pappé, Ilan. 2004. 'The making and unmaking of the Israeli Jewish left'. In *Who's Left in Israel: Radical Political Alternatives for the Future of Israel*, edited by Dan Leon. Brighton: Sussex University Press.

Pappé, Ilan. 2006. *The Ethnic Cleansing of Palestine*. Oxford: Oneworld.

Pappé, Ilan. 2008a. 'Zionism as colonialism: A comparative view of diluted colonialism in Asia and Africa'. *South Atlantic Quarterly* 107 (4): 611–33. https://read.dukeupress.edu/south-atlantic-quarterly/article/107/4/611/3404/Zionism-as-Colonialism-A-Comparative-View-of.

Pappé, Ilan. 2008b. 'The Mukhbarat State of Israel: A state of oppression is not a state of exception'. In *Thinking Palestine*, edited by Ronit Lentin. London: Zed Books.

Pappé, Ilan. 2011. *The Forgotten Palestinians: A History of the Palestinians in Israel*. London: Yale University Press.

Pappé, Ilan. 2015. *Israel and South Africa: The Many Faces of Apartheid*. London: Zed Books.

Pegues, Juliana Hu. 2016. 'Empire, race, and settler colonialism: BDS and contingent solidarities'. *Theory & Event* 9 (6): n.p. https://muse.jhu.edu/article/633272.

Peled, Daniella. 2013. 'Delegitimising the Delegitimisers'. *Jewish Quarterly* 57 (1): 32–3. https://www.tandfonline.com/doi/abs/10.1080/0449010X.2010.10706325.

Peled-Elhanan, Nurit. 2012. *Palestine in Israeli School Books: Ideology and Propaganda in Education*. London: I.B. Tauris.

Peled-Elhanan, Nurit. 2010. 'Legitimation of massacres in Israeli school history books'. *Discourse Society* 21 (4): 377–404. https://www.jstor.org/stable/42889680?seq=1.

Phillips, Matthew. 2011. 'War and Michael Walzer'. *Mondoweiss*. 9 January. https://mondoweiss.net/2011/01/war-and-michael-walzer/.

Philo, Greg, and Berry, Mike. 2004. *Bad News from Israel*. London: Pluto Press.

Philo, Greg, and Berry, Mike. 2011. *More Bad News from Israel*. London: Pluto Press.

Piterberg, Gabriel. 1996. 'Domestic orientalism: The representation of "Oriental" Jews in Zionist/Israeli historiography'. *British Journal of Middle Eastern Studies* 23 (2): 125–45. https://www.jstor.org/stable/195530.

Piterberg, Gabriel. 2001. 'Erasures'. *New Left Review* 10: 31–46. https://newleftreview.org/issues/II10/articles/gabriel-piterberg-erasing-the-palestinians.pdf.

Piterberg, Gabriel. 2008. *The Returns of Zionism: Myths, Politics, and Scholarship in Israel*. London: Verso.

Piterberg, Gabriel. 2010. 'Settlers and their states: A reply to Zeev Sternhell'. *New Left Review* 62: 115–23. https://newleftreview.org/issues/II62/articles/gabriel-piterberg-settlers-and-their-states.pdf.

Plaut, Steven. 2011. 'Israel's tenured extremists'. *Middle East Quarterly* 18 (4): 61–70. https://www.meforum.org/3072/israel-extremist-professors.

Plonski, Sharri. 2018. *Palestinian Citizens of Israel: Power, Resistance and the Struggle for Space*. London: SOAS Palestine Studies Book Series, I.B. Tauris.

Prevent Duty Guidance. [2015] 2019. https://www.gov.uk/government/publications/prevent-duty-guidance.

Probyn, Elspeth. 1996. *Outside Belongings*. London: Routledge.

Puar, Jasbir. 2017. *The Right to Maim: Debility, Capacity, Disability*. Durham: Duke University Press.

Qumsiyeh, Mazin B. 2016. 'A critical and historical assessment of Boycott, Divestment, and Sanctions (BDS) in Palestine'. In *Conflict Transformation and the Palestinians: The Dynamics of Peace and Justice under Occupation*, edited by Alpaslan Ozerdem, Chuck Thiessen and Mufid Qassoum. London: Routledge.

Qumsiyeh, Mazin B. 2010. *Popular Resistance in Palestine: A History of Hope and Empowerment*. London: Pluto Press.

Ravid, Barak. 2010. 'Lieberman presents plans for population exchange at UN'. *Ha'aretz*. 28 September. http://www.haaretz.com/news/diplomacy-defense/lieberman-presents-plans-for-population-exchange-at-un-1.316197.

Raz-Krakotzkin, Amnon. 2011. 'Exile and binationalism: From Gershom Scholem and Hannah Arendt to Edward Said and Mahmoud Darwish'. Carl Heinrich Becker Lecture, EUME. https://www.forum-transregionale-studien.de/en/communication/details/exile-und-binationalism-from-gershom-sholem-and-hannah-arendt-to-edward-said-and-mahmoud-darwish.html. Also available on academia.edu.

Reut Institute. 2010. 'The BDS movement promotes delegitimization against Israel'. http://www.reut-institute.org/Publication.aspx?PublicationId=3868.

Richmond, Oliver P. 2011. 'Critical agency, resistance and a post-colonial civil society'. *Cooperation and Conflict* 46: 419–40. https://doi.org/10.1177/0010836711422416.

Ricoeur, Paul. 1999. 'Memory and forgetting'. In *Questioning Ethics: Contemporary Debates in Philosophy*, edited by in Mark Dooley and Richard Kearney. London: Routledge.

Ricoeur, Paul. 2004. *Memory, History, Forgetting*. London: University of Chicago Press.

Roberts, William Clare, and Schotten, C. Heike. 2019. 'Boycott, Divestment and Sanctions (BDS) and political theory'. *Contemporary Political Theory* 18 (3): 449–52. https://doi.org/10.1057/s41296-019-00331-1.

Robin, Corey. 2019. 'The strategic case for the academic boycott of Israel'. *Contemporary Political Theory* 18 (3): 471–73. https://doi.org/10.1057/s41296-019-00331-1.

Roby, Bryan K. 2015. *The Mizrahi Era of Rebellion: 1948–1966*. New York: Syracuse University Press.

Rosello, Mirielle. 2010. *The Reparative in Narrative: Works of Mourning in Progress*. Liverpool: University of Liverpool Press.

Ross, Alice. 2016. 'Academics criticise anti-radicalisation strategy in open letter'. *The Guardian*. 29 September. https://www.theguardian.com/uk-news/2016/sep/29/academics-criticise-prevent-anti-radicalisation-strategy-open-letter.

Rothberg, Michael. 2009. *Multidirectional Memory: Remembering the Holocaust in the Age of Decolonization*. Stanford, CA: Stanford University Press.

Roy, Arundhati. 2004. 'Help that hinders'. *Le Monde Diplomatique*, English edition. http://mondediplo.com/2004/11/16roy.

Sa'di, Ahmad. H. 2008. 'Remembering Al-nakba in a time of amnesia: On silence, dislocation and time'. *Interventions: International Journal of Postcolonial Studies* 10 (3): 381–99. https://doi.org/10.1080/13698010802445006.

Said, Edward W. 1984. 'Permission to narrate'. *Journal of Palestine Studies* 13 (3): 27–48. https://www.jstor.org/stable/2536688.

Said, Edward W. 1988. 'Identity, negation and violence'. *New Left Review* 171: 46–60. https://newleftreview.org/issues/I171/articles/edward-said-identity-negation-and-violence.

Said, Edward W. 2006. 'A method for thinking about just peace'. In *What Is a Just Peace*, edited by Pierre Allan and Alexis Keller. New York: Oxford University Press.

Salaita, Steven. 2016. *Inter/Nationalism: Decolonizing Native America and Palestine*. Minneapolis: University of Minnesota Press.

Salaita, Steven. 2017. 'American Indian studies and Palestine solidarity: The importance of impetuous definitions'. *Decolonization: Indegeneity, Education & Society* 6 (1): 1–28. https://jps.library.utoronto.ca/index.php/des/article/view/28900.

Salamanca, Omar Jabary, Qato, Mezna, Rabie, Kareem, and Samour, Sobhi. 2012. 'Past is present: Settler colonialism in Palestine'. *Settler Colonial Studies* 2 (1): 1–8. https://doi.org/10.1080/2201473X.2012.10648823.

Sand, Schlomo. 2009. *The Invention of the Jewish People*. London: Verso.

Sandercock, Josie et al. (eds). 2004. *Peace under Fire: Israel/Palestine and the International Solidarity Movement*. London: Verso.

Sayegh, Fayez. [1965] 2012. 'Zionist colonialism in Palestine (1965)'. *Settler Colonial Studies* 2 (1): 206–25. https://doi.org/10.1080/2201473X.2012.10648833.

Schechter, Asher. 2017. ' "We've Won": How Trump empowers Israel's far right'. *World Policy Journal* 34 (1): 33–41. https://muse.jhu.edu/article/652802/pdf.

Schölch, Alexander. 1985. 'The demographic development of Palestine, 1850–1882'. *International Journal of Middle Eastern Studies* 17 (4): 485–505. https://www.jstor.org/stable/163415?seq=1.

Schwietzer, Christine. 2009. 'Civilian peace keeping: Providing protection without sticks and carrots'. In *People Power: Unarmed Resistance and Global Solidarity*, edited by Howard Clark. London: Pluto Press.

Sedek: A Journal on the Ongoing Nakba Journal. 2010. 'Special translated issue'. https://zochrot.org/uploads/uploads/a38b42bf135f097d567f3eed062c39e7.pdf.

Seitz, Charmaine. 2003. 'ISM at the crossroads: The evolution of the International Solidarity Movement'. *Journal of Palestine Studies* 32 (4): 50–67. https://doi.org/10.1525/jps.2003.32.4.50.

Sfard, Michael. 2018. *The Wall and the Gate: Israel, Palestine, and the Legal Battle for Human Rights*. New York: Metropolitan Books.

Shabi, Rachel. 2009. *Not the Enemy: Israel's Jews from Arab Lands*. London: Yale University Press.

Shafir, Gershom. 2005. 'Settler citizenship in the Jewish colonisation of Palestine'. In *Settler Colonialism in the Twentieth Century*, edited by Caroline Elkins and Susan Pedersen. London: Routledge.

Shapiro, Tali. 2010. 'The law of prohibition'. *Pulse Media*. 24 June. https://pulsemedia.org/2010/06/24/law-of-boycott-prohibition/.

Shapiro, Tali. 2013. 'Running with wolves'.. In *Anarchists Against the Wall*, edited by Uri Gordon and Ohal Grietzer. Oakland: AK Press.

Sharoni, Simona, Abdulhadi, Rabab, Al-Ali, Nadje, Eaves, Felicia, Lentin, Ronit and Saddiqi, Dina. 2015. 'Transnational feminist solidarity in times of crisis'. *International Feminist Journal of Politics* 17 (4): 654–70. https://doi.org/10.1080/14616742.2015.1088226

Shavit, Ari. 2004. 'Survival of the fittest: An interview with Benny Morris'. *Ha'aretzMagazine*. 1 July. https://www.haaretz.com/1.5262454.

Shehadeh, Raja. 1988. *Occupier's Law: Israel and the West Bank*. Washington, DC: Institute for Palestine Studies.

Shezaf, Hagar. 2020. 'Israel rejects over 98 percent of Palestinian building permit requests in West Bank's Area C'. *Ha'aretz*. 21 January. https://www.haaretz.com/israel-news/.premium-israel-rejects-98-of-palestinian-building-permit-requests-in-west-bank-s-area-c-1.8403807.

Shihade, Majid. 2016. 'The place of Israel in Asia: Settler colonialism, mobility, memory, and identity among Palestinians in Israel'. *Settler Colonial Studies* 6 (2): 133–41. https://doi.org/10.1080/2201473X.2015.1024379.

Shihade, Majid. 2015a. 'Global Israel: Settler colonialism, mobility, and rupture'. *Borderlands: e-journal* 14 (1): 1–16. https://go.gale.com/

ps/anonymous?id=GALE%7CA458263304&sid=googleScholar&v=2.1&it=r&linkaccess=abs&issn=14470810&p=AONE&sw=w.

Shohat, Ella. 2017. *On the Arab-Jew, Palestine, and Other Displacements*. London: Pluto Press.

Shulman, David. 2007. *Hope in Dark Times: Working for Peace in Israel and Palestine*. London: University of Chicago Press.

Silver, Charlotte. 2011. 'Tristan Anderson civil suit delayed as more evidence emerges'. *Electronic Intifada*. 3 December. https://electronicintifada.net/content/tristan-anderson-civil-suit-delayed-new-evidence-emerges/10649.

Simpson, Audra. 2017. 'The ruse of consent and the anatomy of "refusal": Cases from indigenous North America and Australia'. *Postcolonial Studies* 20 (1): 18–33. https://doi.org/10.1080/13688790.2017.1334283.

Singh, Jakeet. 2019. 'Power, settler colonialism, and the role of external actors'. *Contemporary Political Theory* 18 (3): 468–71. https://doi.org/10.1057/s41296-018-0277-5.

Smith, Andrea. 2012. 'Indigeneity, settler colonialism, white supremacy'. In *Racial Formation in the Twenty-First Century*, edited by Daniel Martinez HoSang, Oneka LaBennett and Laura Pulido. Berkeley: University of California Press.

Smith, Jackie, et al. 1997. *Transnational Social Movements and Global Politics: Solidarity beyond the State*. New York: Syracusse University Press.

Smith, Malcolm. 2000. *Britain and 1940: History, Myth, and Popular Memory*. London: Routledge.

Snitz, Kobi. 2004. 'On recent Palestinian popular resistance and its Israeli support'. *We Are All Anarchists Against the Wall!* http://www.fdca.it/fdcaen/press/pamphlets/waaaatw.htm#On%20recent%20Palestinian%20Popular%20Resistance%20and%20its%20Israeli%20Support.

Snitz, Kobi. 2013. 'Tear gas and tea'. In *Anarchists Against the Wall*, edited by Uri Gordon and Ohal Grietzer. Oakland: AK Press.

Speck, Andreas. 2012. 'Reflections on Cynthia Cockburn's anti-militarism'. Presentation at anti-Militarism book launch, Housmans Bookshop, London, UK.

Stamatopoulou-Robbins, Sophia. 2008. 'The joys and dangers of solidarity in Palestine: Prosthetic engagement in an age of reparations'. *CR: The New Centennial Review* 8 (2): 111–60. https://muse.jhu.edu/article/255108/pdf.

Stanley, Liz. 2017. *The Racialising Process: Whites Writing Whiteness in Letters, South Africa 1770s-1970s*. Edinburgh: X Press.

Stasiulis, Daiva, and Yuval-Davis, Nira (eds). 1995. *Unsettling Settler Societies: Articulations of Gender, Race, Ethnicity and Class*. London: Sage.

Svirsky, Marcelo. 2012. *Arab-Jewish Activism in Israel-Palestine*. Farnham: Ashgate.

Svirsky, Marcelo. 2014a. 'The collaborative struggle and the permeability of settler colonialism'. *Settler Colonial Studies* 4 (4): 327–32. https://doi.org/10.1080/2201473X.2014.911649.

Svirsky, Marcelo. 2014b. 'On the study of collaborative struggles in settler societies'. *Settler Colonial Studies* 4 (4): 434–49. https://doi.org/10.1080/2201473X.2014.911648.

Svirsky, Marcelo. 2014c. *After Israel: Towards Cultural Transformation*. London: Zed Books.

Svirsky, Marcelo. 2017. 'Resistance is a structure not an event'. *Settler Colonial Studies* 7 (1): 1–21. https://doi.org/10.1080/2201473X.2016.1141462.

Tabar, Linda. 2017. 'From third world internationalism to "the internationals": The transformation of solidarity with Palestine". *Third World Quarterly* 38 (2): 414–35. https://doi.org/10.1080/01436597.2016.1142369.

Tabar, Linda, and Desai, Chandni. 2017. 'Decolonization is a global project: From Palestine to the Americas'. *Decolonization: Indigeneity, Education & Society* 6 (1): i–xix. https://jps.library.utoronto.ca/index.php/des/article/view/28899.

Tarachansky, Lia. 2011. *Seven Deadly Myths*. http://sevendeadlymyths.webs.com/.

Tarrow, Sidney G. 2005. *The New Transnational Activism*. Cambridge: Cambridge University Press.

Tarrow, Sidney G. 2011. *Power in Movement: Social Movements and Contentious Politics*. Cambridge: Cambridge University Press.

Tatour, Lana. 2016a. 'Domination and resistance in liberal settler colonialism: Palestinians in Israel between the homeland and the transnational'. Doctoral Thesis, University of Warwick.

Tatour, Lana. 2016b. 'The Israeli left: Part of the problem or the solution? A response to Giulia Daniele'. *Global Discourse* 6 (3): 487–92. https://doi.org/10.1080/23269995.2016.1199474.

Tatour, Lana. 2019. 'New law old news for Palestinian apartheid'. *Eureka Street* 29: 3. https://www.eurekastreet.com.au/article/new-law-old-news-for-palestinian-apartheid.

Taylor, Keeanga-Yamahtta. 2016. *From #BlackLivesMatter to Black Liberation*. Chicago: Haymarket Books.

The Washington Post, Times Herald. 1969. 'Golda Meir Scorns Soviets'. Acquired from ProQuest Historical Newspapers, *Washington Post* (1877–1994).

Tharoor, Ishaan. 2014. 'Map: The countries that recognize Palestine as a state'. *Washington Post*. 7 November. http://www.washingtonpost.com/blogs/worldviews/wp/2014/11/07/map-the-countries-that-recognize-palestine-as-a-state/.

Till, Karen E. 2008. 'Artistic and activist memory-work: Approaching place-based practice'. *Memory Studies* 1 (1): 99–113. https://doi.org/10.1177/1750698007083893.

Tilly, Virginia. 2005. *The One State Solution: A Breakthrough for Peace in the Israeli Palestinian Deadlock*. Manchester: Manchester University Press.

Topolski, Anya. 2010. 'Peacekeeping without banisters: The need for new practices that go beyond just war theory'. In *At War for Peace*, edited by Mohammadbagher Forough. Boston: Brill. https://doi.org/10.1163/9781848880351_006.

Trudeau, Daniel. 2006. 'Politics of belonging in the construction of landscapes: Place-making, boundary-drawing, and exclusion'. *Cultural Geographies* 13 (3): 421–43. https://doi.org/10.1191/1474474006eu366oa.

Tuck, Eve, and Yang, K. Wayne. 2012. 'Decolonization is not a metaphor'. *Decolonization: Indigeneity, Education & Society* 1 (1): 1–40. https://jps.library.utoronto.ca/index.php/des/article/view/18630.

Turner, Mandy. 2015. 'Creating a counterhegemonic praxis: Jewish-Israeli activists and the challenge to Zionism'. *Conflict, Security & Development* 15 (5): 549–74. https://doi.org/10.1080/14678802.2015.1100018.

United Nations: The Question of Palestine. 2018. 'Gaza "unliveable", UN special rapporteur for the situation of human rights in the OPT tells third committee – press release (excerpts)'. https://www.un.org/unispal/document/gaza-unliveable-un-special-rapporteur-for-the-situation-of-human-rights-in-the-opt-tells-third-committee-press-release-excerpts/.

United Nations. 1973. 'International convention on the suppression and punishment of the crime of apartheid'. https://www.un.org/en/genocideprevention/documents/atrocity-crimes/Doc.10_International%20Convention%20on%20the%20Suppression%20and%20Punishment%20of%20the%20Crime%20of%20Apartheid.pdf.

United Nations Security Council. 'Resolution 242 (1967) of 22 November 1967'. https://unispal.un.org/unispal.nsf/0/7D35E1F729DF491C85256EE700686136.

UNCHRC. 2020. 'Israeli annexation plans would lead to "cascade of bad human rights consequences", says UN expert'. 1 May. https://www.ohchr.org/EN/NewsEvents/Pages/DisplayNews.aspx?NewsID=25857&LangID=E.

UNCTAD. 2015. 'Occupied Palestinian Territory slides into recession, Gaza becoming uninhabitable'. https://unctad.org/en/pages/newsdetails.aspx?OriginalVersionID=1068.

UNOCHA: Occupied Palestinian Territory. 2019. 'West Bank demolitions and displacement: August 2019'. https://www.ochaopt.org/content/west-bank-demolitions-and-displacement-august-2019.

Valji, Nahla. 2003. 'South Africa: No justice without reparation'. OpenDemocracy.net. 1 July. https://www.opendemocracy.net/en/article_1326jsp/.

Veracini, Lorenzo. 2007. 'Settler colonialism and decolonisation'. *Borderlands e-journal* 6 (2): 1–30. https://ro.uow.edu.au/lhapapers/1337/.

Veracini, Lorenzo. 2010. *Settler Colonialism: A Theoretical Overview*. London: Palgrave Macmillan.

Veracini, Lorenzo. 2013. 'The other shift: Settler colonialism, Israel and the Occupation'. *Journal of Palestine Studies* 42 (2): 26–42. https://doi.org/10.1525/jps.2013.42.2.26.

Veracini, Lorenzo. 2017. 'Decolonizing settler colonialism: Kill the settler in him and save the man'. *American Indian Culture and Research Journal* 41 (1): 1–18. https://meridian.allenpress.com/aicrj/article-abstract/41/1/1/211843/Decolonizing-Settler-Colonialism-Kill-the-Settler?redirectedFrom=fulltext.

Wagner, Roy. 2013. 'Fear and loathing at the central bus stop'. In *Anarchists Against the Wall*, edited by Uri Gordon and Ohal Grietzer, 60–9. Oakland: AK Press.

Walby, Sylvia. 2009. *Globalization and Inequalities: Complexity and Contested Modernities*. London: Sage.

Walia, Harsha. n.d. 'Moving beyond a politics of solidarity towards a practice of decolonization'. *Colours of Resistance Archive*. http://www.coloursofresistance.org/769/moving-beyond-a-politics-of-solidarity-towards-a-practice-of-decolonization/.

Walia, Harsha. 2013. *Undoing Border Imperialism*. Edinburgh: AK Press.

Waxman, Dov. 2016. 'Is Israeli democracy in danger'. *Current History* 115 (785): 360–2. https://doi.org/10.1525/curh.2016.115.785.360.

Waziyatawin. 2012. 'Malice enough in their hearts and courage enough in ours: Reflections on US indigenous and Palestinian experiences under Occupation'. *Settler Colonial Studies* 2 (1): 172–89. https://doi.org/10.1080/2201473X.2012.10648831.

Weheliye, Alexander G. 2014. *Habeas Viscus: Racializing Assemblages, Biopolitics, and Black Feminist Theories of the Human*. London: Duke University Press.

Weizman, Elian. 2017. 'Decolonising Israeli society? Resistance to Zionism as an educative practice'. *Ethnicities* 17 (4): 574–97. https://doi.org/10.1177/1468796816666593.

Weizman, Eyal. 2007. *Hollow Land: Israel's Architecture of Occupation*. London: Verso.

Weizman, Eyal. 2011. *The Least of All Possible Evils: Humanitarian Violence from Arendt to Gaza*. London: Verso.

Who Profits From the Occupation. 'Find a company'. http://www.whoprofits.org.

Wiles, Rich (ed.). 2013. *Generation Palestine: Voices from the Boycott, Divestment and Sanctions Movement*. London: Pluto Press.

Winstanley, Asa, and Barat, Frank. 2011. *Corporate Complicity in Israel's Occupation: Evidence from the London Session of the Russell Tribunal.* London: Pluto Press.

Wolfe, Patrick. 1999. *Settler Colonialism and the Transformation of Anthropology: The Politics and Poetics of an Ethnographic Event.* London: Cassell.

Wolfe, Patrick. 2006. 'Settler colonialism and the elimination of the native'. *Journal of Genocide Research* 8 (4): 387–410. https://doi.org/10.1080/14623520601056240.

Wolfe, Patrick. 2012. 'New Jews for old: Settler state formation and the impossibility of Zionism: In memory of Edward W. Said'. *Arena Journal* 37/38: 285–321. https://search.informit.com.au/documentSummary;dn=641411011826029;res=IELAPA.

Wolfe, Patrick. 2016a. *Traces of History: Elementary Structures of Race.* London: Verso.

Wolfe. Patrick (ed.) 2016b. *The Settler Complex: Recuperating Binarism in Colonial Studies.* Los Angeles, California: UCLA American Indian Studies Centre.

Yiftachel, Oren. 2010. '"Ethnocracy": The politics of Judaizing Israel/Palestine'. In *Across the Wall: Narratives of Israeli-Palestinian History*, edited by Jamil Hilal and Ilan Pappé. London: I.B. Tauris.

Yoffie. Eric H. 2020. 'Opinion: U.S. Jews are clear: We won't back Bibi's conspiracies, colonial inclinations or corruption'. *Ha'aretz.* 6 July. https://www.haaretz.com/us-news/.premium-u-s-jews-are-clear-we-won-t-back-bibi-s-conspiracies-colonialism-or-corruption-1.8971350.

Yuval-Davis, Nira. 2006. 'Belonging and the politics of belonging'. *Patterns of Prejudice* 40 (3): 197–214. https://doi.org/10.1080/00313220600769331.

Yuval-Davis, Nira. 2011. *The Politics of Belonging: Intersectional Contestations.* London: Sage.

Zertal, Idith. 2005. *Israel's Holocaust and the Politics of Nationhood.* Cambridge: Cambridge University Press.

Zochrot. 2005. 'High Court petition on Canada Park'. https://www.zochrot.org/en/article/52089.

Zochrot. 2006a. 'Response of the Occupied Territories Military Commander to Zochrot's Canada Park petition'. https://www.zochrot.org/en/article/52097.

Zochrot. 2006b. 'JNF's response to Zochrot's Canada Park petition'. https://zochrot.org/en/article/52093.

Zochrot. 2008. 'Annual report'. https://zochrot.org/en/yearlyReport/52414.

Zochrot. 2009. 'Annual report'. https://www.zochrot.org/en/yearlyReport/52714.

Zochrot. 2012a. 'The Cape Town document'. https://zochrot.org/en/event/54538.

Zochrot. 2012b. 'Towards a common archive'. https://zochrot.org/en/gallery/54187.

Zreik, Raef. 2008. 'The resistance of the exception: Some remarks on the story of Israeli constitutionalism'. In *Thinking Palestine*, edited by Ronit Lentin. London: Zed Books.

Zureik, Elia. 2001. 'Constructing Palestine through surveillance practices'. *British Journal of Middle Eastern Studies* 28 (2): 205–27. https://www.tandfonline.com/doi/abs/10.1080/13530190120083086/.

Index

Abu-Lughod, L. 50–1
Abunimah, A. 70, 73, 79
abuses 69. *see also* violations
academic boycott 39
Agamben, G. 47
Algeria 10–11
Anarchists Against the Wall (AATW) 5, 74, 88–9
anti-Black racism 3
Anti-Boycott Law 109
Apartheid practices 25
Arab minority 52
Ashkenazi-dominated critical activism 6
Ashkenazi middle class 6
Australia 29, 37–8
automatic citizenship 26

BADIL 55, 58, 60
Barghouti, O. 71
Bedouin Palestinians 9
binationalism
 of Brit Shalom 72
 implications of 71
 Jewish-Israeli proponents of 72
 of newcomers 72
 as a process of decolonization 12–15
 as settler decolonization 65–83
 of settlers 72
binational statement 69–75
Birth of the Palestinian Refugee Problem, The (Morris) 48
Black Lives Matter 115
Bot, M. 114–15
Boycott, Divestment and Sanctions (BDS) 7, 12–14, 19, 24, 25, 29, 69, 104
British Labour Party 100
Bruyneel, K. 29
Buber, M. 72
Butler, J. 76, 90
Buttigieg, J. A. 102

Canada 29
citizenship (ezrahut) 25, 26
 automatic 26
 cultural, social and political 114
 denial of basic 4
 equal 99, 114, 120
 histories of 54
 human rights and human security 111
 litmus test for rights 111
 modern 27
 racialized migrants 4
 rights 27, 59
 secular democratic principles of 75
 stratified hierarchy of 30
 threats to 111
civil society 99, 100–8
Clarno, A. 24
class-based solidarity 3
Cockburn, C. 32
Cocks, J. 12
cohabitation 5, 15
colonialism. *see also* settler colonialism
 characteristics of 76
 for decolonization 7
 European 1
 histories of 116
 Israeli 2, 35
 legitimacy of 116
 in Palestine-Israel 5, 81
 pure 10
 responsibility/complicity in 8
 settler 1–2, 8, 10–11
 unsettling settler 35–40
colonization
 of Arab lands 7
 articulations of resistance to 95
 benefits from 89
 co-resistance against 12
 defined 8
 human rights violations 113
 indigenous resistance to 20

of Palestinian land 1, 31
  settler 9, 73, 76, 80
  of the West Bank 9
Corbyn, J. 100
Corrie, R. 68, 95
counter-terrorism 112
criminalization 3
crisis 24
cross-border solidarity 36

Davies, R. 51
Davis, U. 73, 75
decolonial futurities 36
decolonial scholarship 36. *see also* scholarship
decolonial solidarity 3, 7, 93–6
decolonization 6–12
  as an internal process 75
  binationalism as a process of 12–15
  indigenous-led struggles 7
  Israeli settler-activist-scholarship 7
  for latter organization 74
  Palestinian struggle for 19
  possibilities for 77
  self-determination in 65–6
  settler 72
  theorized 7
  of Zionism 15
decolonizing settler memory 53–62
delegitimation campaign 112–17
delegitimizing delegitimizers 99–117
  civil society 100–8
  delegitimizing democracy 109–12
  overview 99–100
  transnationalizing the delegitimation campaign 112–17
delegitimizing democracy 109–12
de-racination 3
disaster capitalism 22
dispossessive settler colonialism 73. *see also* colonialism
Duffield, M. 101

Egypt 70
Electronic Intifada (Abunimah) 70
elitism 6
equal citizenship 99, 114, 120
ethnic cleansing 49

Ethnic Cleansing of Palestine, The (Pappé) 48
European colonialism 1. *see also* colonialism
European-heritage Jewish population 6
exogenous agency 8
exogenous labour 11
exploitation labour 3

Farsakh, L. 73
Feldman, J. 45
Fiala, A. 32
Finland 67
French Algeria 10

Gaza Strip 5, 9, 13–14, 21, 24, 51, 68, 85
Germany 67
Goldberg, D. 29
Gordon, N. 90, 110
Gordon, U. 74, 88
Gramsci, A. 99, 102
grassroots solidarity 67
Grietzer, O. 88

Haifa Declaration 24
Halper, J. 8, 65–7, 69, 79–80
Hammami, R. 89, 94
Hasan Bek Mosque 51
Hebrew cultural 65–6
Hever, S. 23
human rights 113–16
  abuses 69
  active delegitimation of 110
  advocates 111
  committees 67
  delegitimation 111
  movements 103
  norms 110
  organizations 109, 110
  regional confederation 70
  security of 105
  violations 39, 69, 105, 113

indigenous scholarship 37. *see also* scholarship
inequality 24
intercommunal violence 77
Interim Agreement 86

International Holocaust Remembrance Alliance (IHRA) 113
Internationalism 104
international media 19
International Solidarity Movement (ISM) 88–9
Israel 70
  BDS against 7, 12
  borders 3, 9, 67
  colonialism 2, 40, 53, 111, 120
  establishment of 1, 9
  groups 5
  hegemonic narrative of 43
  human rights abuses 69
  Independence Day 52
  as a Jewish state 24
  military occupation 3
  Palestinian citizens of 4
  parliamentary politics 2
  settler-colonial project 20
  state narrative 20
  state violence 19
  technologies 2
  voluntary expulsion 26
  war economy 23
Israeli Committee Against House Demolitions (ICAHD) 5, 8, 65–83
  activities 66
  activities in Occupied Territories 67
  alternative education tours 66
  binational proposal 79
  binational statement 69–76
  boycott statement 69
  defined 66
  ECOSOC Special Consultative Status award 66
  Nobel Peace Prize 66
  Olive Branch Award 66
  one-state statement 73
  peace centre 67
  political analysis 66
  practical solidarity 66
  role of 67
  sister organizations 67
  transnational advocacy 66
Israeli Defence Forces (IDF) 30–1
Israeli in Palestine, An (Halper) 65
Israeli labour 23
Israeli Land Authority 49

Israeli settler colony 19–41
  apartheid 24–9
  from militarism to refusal 30–5
  overview 19–24
  unsettling settler colonialism 35–40

Jewish 9–10
Jewish-Israeli
  activists 29, 35
  community 75
  democratic regime 29
  history 75
  majority of 29
  notion of 77
  public 15
  self-determination 75
  settler-colonial framework 16
  settler community 75
  solidarity actions of 35
Jewish majority population 2
Jewish National Fund (JNF) 25, 28, 49, 54
Jewish-only labour 10
Jewish settler-colonial 4–5
Jews 2
Jordan 70
Judaism 3
Judaization 9

Kaldor, M. 100–2
Karatzogianni, A. 20
Khalidi, R. 85
Khalidi, W. 48
Khoury-Bisharat, H. 110
Kidron, P. 32
'Kirby definition' 71
Klein, N. 22, 24
Kook, R. 107

labour
  cheap 10–11
  exogenous 11
  exploitation 3
  Israeli 23
  Jewish-only 10
  land *versus* 10
  Native land 4
  Palestinian 24
  Palestinian indigenous 2
  plentiful and cheaper 10

Lahav, H. 30
Lavie, S. 3, 6
Law of Return 25
Lebanon 51, 70
legitimate scholarship 112. *see also* scholarship
Lemish, D. 32
Lentin, R. 29, 56
Lentin cautions 2
Likud Party 3
Lintl, P. 107

marginality 6
marginalization 24
Mas'ha camp 88
Meir, G. 20, 43
militarism to refusal 30–5
Mills, C. 47
Mizrahi Jewish population 2
Mizrahi-led anti-discrimination movement 6
Mizrahim 3–4, 31
Mizrahi migrants 8
Mizrahi population 2–3
mobilization
  advocacy and 35–6
  BDS 35–6
  political 91
  public 49
  settler-colonial framework 29
  of vulnerability 91
modern citizenship 27
Morrar, A. 94
Morris, B. 44, 48

Na'amati, G. 95
Nakba 2, 9, 15, 21, 35, 123n4
Nakba: Palestine, 1948 and the Claims of Memory (Abu-Lughod) 50
nationality (le'um) 25
Nation State Law 3
Negev/Naqab 9, 67
neoliberal apartheid 24

Occupied Palestinian Territories (OPTs) 21, 23–4, 27, 68
Occupied Territories 24–5
  administration and policing of 30
  destructive operations in 68
  ethnonational segregation 26
  ICAHD's activities in 67
  Palestinians in 30
  policy of closure in 68
  sovereignty in 46
Occupied West Bank 5, 9
One Country (Abunimah) 70–1
One Democratic State Campaign 80–1
organized violence 19–20
Oslo Accords 10, 13–14, 21, 50, 85–6, 106

Palestine 2
Palestine in Israeli School Books (Peled-Elhanan) 34
Palestine-Israel
  critical decolonial activism 5–6
  decolonization 1, 5, 6–12
  geopolitics of 1
  intercultural cohabitation in 5
  Jewish privilege 8
  settler colonialism in 5
  settler-colonial project in 6
  as a settler-colonial relation 8
  settler–indigenous relations in 1
  sociopolitical relations in 1
Palestine Liberation Organization (PLO) 21
Palestinian anti-colonial scholarship 1
Palestinian Authority (PA) 27, 86
Palestinian indigenous labour 2
Palestinian labour 24
Palestinian labour law 23
Palestinian liberation-focused scholarship 36
Palestinian population 1
Palestinian refugees 51, 54
  diaspora 70, 80
  plight of 44
  PLO 21
  problem 44
  return of 7–8, 56–60, 75
  right of return of 9, 25, 29, 45, 55, 66, 69–70, 123n5
  second and third generation 51
  tertiary displacement 59–60
Palestinian scholarship 48
Palestinian Solidarity Movement (PSM) 104

Palestinian terrorism 19
Palestinian Trade Unions 23
Pallister-Wilkins, P. 89
Pappé, I. 44, 48–9
paradigm
   settler-colonial 11
   two-state 12, 21, 82
   zero-sum 11
Peace Under Fire (Sandercock) 88
Pegues, J. H. 39
Peled-Elhanan, N. 34, 52, 56
Perugini, N. 90
political mobilization 91
political violence 19
poverty 3
practical solidarity 5
present absentees 52
Prison Notebooks (Gramsci) 99
Probyn, E. 78
progressive scholarship 99
public mobilization 49
Public War, Private Conscience (Fiala) 32
pure colonialism 10

race-class-gender conscious analysis 6
Raz-Krakotzkin, A. 14
refugee 1. *see also* Palestinian refugees
   absorption of 60
   diaspora 59
   financial and practical provisions 59
   Gaza's residents 61
   hierarchy of 61
   host states 59
   in Lebanon 61
   right of return 63
   role of Gaza Strip 51
   village 52–3
Remnants of Auschwitz (Agamben) 47
responsibility 47
Rhodesia/Zimbabwe 11
Ricoeur, P. 47, 49
Robinson, A. 20
Roy, A. 102

Said, E. 19, 43
Sandercock, J. 88
Sanders, B. 100
scholarship
   decolonial 36

   indigenous 37
   legitimate 112
   Palestinian 48
   Palestinian anti-colonial 1
   Palestinian liberation-focused 36
   progressive 99
   proliferation of 38
   settler-activist 7
   settler-colonial framework in 38
Scholem, G. 71–2
securitization 24
settler-activist-scholarship 7
settler colonialism 1–2. *see also* colonialism
   characteristic of 10
   decolonial futurities 36
   decolonization and 39
   decolonizing 11
   dispossessive 73
   hegemonic acceptance 40
   historical and contemporary 36
   internalized logics of 37
   Israeli 2, 40, 53, 111, 120
   Jewish diasporic 66
   nature of 8
   in Palestine-Israel 5, 81
   possession of the land 4
   transnational history of 105
   triumphant project 37
   unsettling 35–40
   Zionist 82
settler-colonial paradigm 11
settler-colonial regimes 29
Settler Colonial Theory (SCT) 36–8
Shafir, G. 10
Singh, J. 39
Smith, J. 103
social mobility 3
solidarity
   acknowledgement of 7
   act of 33
   class-based 3
   cross-border 36
   decolonial 3, 5, 7, 16, 93–6
   expression of 39
   with Gaza 67
   grassroots 67
   practical 5
   practice of 39, 66
   rearticulation of 36, 38

transnational 36
  witnessing intensifying 17
South Africa 11, 25, 58, 71
Speck, A. 32
supporting terrorism 108
surplus humanity 24
Svirsky, M. 74
Syria 51, 70

Tatour, L. 3
terrorism
  anti-Semitism and 100
  concept of 19
  counter 112
  fear of 92
  Palestinian 19
  political violence 19
  supporting 108
Till, K. E. 54
transnationalizing the delegitimation campaign 112–17
transnational solidarity 36
Truth and Reconciliation Commission (TRC) 58
Tuck, E. 7
two-state paradigm 12, 21, 82

UK 67
unchosen proximity 5. *see also* cohabitation
UN General Assembly Resolution 181 (II) 85
unintended consequences 110
United States 13, 17, 67, 108
  as an European-dominated settler colonies 3, 8
  civil rights for African Americans in 11
  Democratic Party presidential candidacy in 100
  enslaved Africans in 8
  ICAHD 67
  indigenous people 11
  Indigenous Studies Association in 39
  Jewish-identified citizens in 115
  military aid budget 59
  Right of Return Conference 58
  settler-colonial regimes 29
  state and federal level in 114
UN Security Council Resolution 13
unsettling settler colonialism 35–40

Veracini, L. 8, 36
violations
  endless cycle of 20
  human rights 39, 69, 105, 113
  intercommunal 77
  organized 19–20
  political 19
  symbolic and/or real 77–8
vulnerability
  articulates 90
  mobilization of 90–1, 94
  political action experiences 91
  political mobilization 91
  politics of 90
  as a politics of decolonial solidarity 85–97
  precarity presupposes 91
  role in non-violent resistance 90
  violent assault 94

Weheliye, A. G. 29
Weizman, E. 107
West Bank 9–10, 13–14, 21–2, 51, 68, 85
West Bank Separation Wall 19, 22, 68, 87–90
witness
  defined 47–50
  as resistance 50–3
Wolfe, P. 1, 3–4

Yang, K. 7
Yuval-Davis, N. 78

zero-sum paradigm 11
Zionism 2, 15, 76
Zionist settler-colonial project 2
Zochrot (Israeli group) 5, 8, 35, 67, 82
  BADIL and 58
  commemorative activism 45, 54–6, 62, 75
  engages act 55
  founders 60
  geopolitical space 55
  Israeli organizations 46, 53
  Nakba 43–63
  public conference 55
  remembrance activities 62
  Supreme Court lawsuit 54
  website 56–7

Printed in the USA
CPSIA information can be obtained
at www.ICGtesting.com
LVHW050542300723
753749LV00006B/214